MAKING MEANING

 How Successful Businesses Deliver
Meaningful Customer Experiences

Steve Diller

Nathan Shedroff

Darrel Rhea

New
Riders

MAKING MEANING: *How Successful Businesses Deliver Meaningful Customer Experiences*

Steve Diller, Nathan Shedroff, and Darrel Rhea

New Riders
1249 Eighth Street
Berkeley, CA 94710
510/524-2178
800/283-9444
510/524-2221 (fax)

Find us on the World Wide Web at: www.newriders.com

To report errors, please send a note to errata@peachpit.com

New Riders is an imprint of Peachpit, a division of Pearson Education

ISBN 0–321–37409–6

9 8 7 6 5 4 3 2 1

Printed in the United States of America

Interior design: Joan Olson

Acknowledgments

The authors would like to offer a heartfelt thanks to the many people who made this book possible. It has truly been a privilege for us to work side by side with outstanding people from the world's best companies, people who helped shape our perspective while working to innovate products, services, and brands. Specifically, thank you to those clients who gave us the opportunity to learn and invent, becoming our friends in the process. We have also benefited from our collaborations with the many other business, technology, design, and product development consultants that who have leveraged and challenged our ideas along the way.

This book benefited from the strong support of Cheskin Principals principals Davis Masten and Christopher Ireland, who have played unparalleled roles in the lives of all three of us as partners, mentors, and friends. It also benefitted from the a large number of people both inside and outside Cheskin, who listened to our ideas, put themselves through painful readings of half-developed drafts, and came back with gold. Our advisors on this project, Maya Babish, Terri Ducay, Lynda Firey-Oldroyd, Tony Golsby-Smith, Jennifer Gray, Ric Grefe, Denise Klarquist, Brenda Laurel, Clement Mok, and Lee Shupp are not only brilliant innovators, but generous and valued friends as well.

The three of us would also like to thank our editor, Marjorie Baer, and all of the people at New Riders who helped bring this book to life, including Michael Nolan who brought us to New Riders in the first place.

Many thanks to my co-workers in our Experience Design Studio who were a constant source of great ideas, enthusiastically brainstorming on just about anything, even as deadlines loomed in their own work. I also would like to acknowledge a few friends, many of whom began as clients, who contributed mightily to the thinking that contributed to this book: Cindy Butner, Michael Caplan, Steve O'Neal, George Scribner, Robin Seymour, and Margaret Sullivan. Finally, my thanks to my partner, Ira Johnson, who makes meaning in life a day-to-day reality for me.

                                                              —*Steve*

The process of creating this book has opened my eyes beyond the idea of experience to the appreciation of meaning. The meanings I experience are the direct result of the many friends and family around me, creating and supporting them in cooperation, and too numerous to list completely. This includes the many students and fellow professors I've encountered through my teaching and studies.

                                                            —*Nathan*

Thank you to my many friends here at home and abroad, who enthusiastically supported me in this effort. My co-workers at Cheskin have created an environment for collaboration and learning that has inspired me to continually grow, and this book is direct outgrowth of their commitment to develop the best and most rigorous thinking. And, a very special thank you to my parents, who believed in me, no matter what, and to my wife, Nancy, and our children, Casey, Randy, Megan and Claire, who taught me to understand life's ultimate meaning.

                                                             —*Darrel*

Contents

Introduction

Meaning: The Heart and Soul of Innovation

E very morning, all around the world, billions of people wake up and go to work. For some, this may mean walking out into the fields adjacent to their home. For others, it may take an hour-long commute to reach their cubicle on the 50th floor. Regardless of the path, all are moving toward activities that define a large part of who they are. Whether you are a farmer or fund manager, the tasks you do, the responsibilities you hold, the relationships and decisions you make, all express parts of your identity and define you in significant ways. Because of this connection, most of us care about the meaning of what we do.

That said, this is not a book about finding your soul in the workplace; many others have spoken to that issue. It's a straightforward business book with a straightforward capitalistic goal: to encourage businesses to create more value by adopting a process that deliberately places meaning at the center of innovation. What we present here is a model for innovation that influences the wider commercial environment in which we all interact. We envision a time when customers increasingly make their purchase decisions based on deeply valued meanings that companies evoke for them through their products and services—in other words, meaningful consumption—as opposed to simply responding based on features, price, brand identity, and emotional pitches. We hope to persuade business leaders that combining and integrating the power of invention, design, and marketing to create meaningful experiences for their customers provides a blueprint to achieving sustained, stable growth.

This is a recipe for a healthy business in any economic climate, but in today's volatile environment, where shareholder value can evaporate more quickly than it can be built, we believe it is both a timely and a reasonable pursuit. If you innovate with an eye to what it meaningful in your customers' lives, your products and services are more likely to be adopted and retained, not tossed aside when the next new sensation arrives. If you identify the core meanings that your product, service, or brand convey, you are more capable of translating the experience into multiple cultures—again, a timely and reasonable pursuit, given our increasingly globalized economy. And if you approach innovation with meaning at the center of your process, you are better able to foster open and transparent collaboration among departments and functions. This saves costs, saves time, and produces real value for your customer, your shareholders, and the people with whom you work.

For customers, the value is conveyed through a positive product experience and lasting brand loyalty. For shareholders, it comes in the form of ongoing profitability and a return on their financial investment in the company. For employees, the value of their work is also expressed as a return on their investment—of time and creativity, labor and a commitment to quality, and their identification with and loyalty to the company and its offerings.

We write this book in the tradition of Louis Cheskin, who in 1945, embarked on what became a life-long obsession to understand the elements of meaning embedded in the relationship between companies and their customers. Using the emerging discipline of psychology, he helped some of this country's most prominent businessmen (and they were all men at that time) to rethink and redesign their products. He helped Marlboro find its masculinity, margarine find its true color (yellow).

Some 50-odd years later, the company he founded is a thriving consultancy that continues to help companies build meaningful connections with their customers. The designers, researchers, anthropologists, and marketers who work at Cheskin, many of whom contributed to this book, continue to find meaning in their work; both for themselves and for the hundreds of clients who partner with us to build greater meaning into their products, services and brands. *Making Meaning* shares our perspective gained over the course of more than 30 years advising companies on innovation in product development, design, and marketing. Separately and together, we three authors counseled hundreds of companies on both strategies and implementations that help create better experiences for their customers and audiences.

"Experience" is a term that has spread throughout the business world with increasingly frequency over the course of the past decade—somewhat to the detriment of the concept. Phrases like "experience marketing," "experience branding," "experience design," "experience economy," and "360 degree branding" (a form of experience design) have proliferated, reflecting a recognition that customers relate to products and services in ways that go beyond their perception of the functional value of those offerings. Some of companies are well recognized for the success of their total customer experience—Disney and Apple, for example—and in fact acknowledge the power and value of this approach. Others are less obvious, such as John Deere, General Motors, and Procter & Gamble, yet they all identify experience as a significant factor affecting their financial performance. For all the interest in the concept of the customer experience, however, there's been little concrete discussion of how it's achieved. Even some of the companies that have succeeded at it seem to have gotten there by accident or, in rare instances, been led to their successes by the leadership of a marketing genius, such as Steve Jobs.

Our own work in the field has led us to the conviction that for companies to achieve enduring competitive advantage through experience design, their innovations cannot be based simply on novelty. Increasingly, they must address their customers' essential human need for meaning. To do this, companies must first understand the role that meaning plays in people's lives, how products and services can evoke meaning, and then how to identify the core meanings they should target with their own offerings. For companies facing both globalization and the end of the mass market, "making meaning" is one of very few strategies that will work.

In this book, we observe, define, and describe the phenomenon of the meaningful customer experience. Where Louis Cheskin drew almost exclusively from psychology, we add insights from cultural anthropology and contextual design. In this book we briefly wrestle with defining both "experience" and "meaning" in the context of business innovation. As you might imagine, these are slippery terms, but we provide ample illustration of what we mean—some from our own client work, some from other companies. We offer you a list of types of meaning our work has led us to find are most valuable to people, but we'll also encourage you to add your own. And, importantly, we offer practical strategies for turning your business into a "meaning business," focusing on the roles, tools, and process of identifying, designing, delivering, and maintaining meaningful experiences. We show you how meaning can be the engine behind innovation and an organization's strategic plan, as well as a way of unifying vision and communicating it to everyone in an organization clearly and simply—whether you're selling software or soft drinks, or something that doesn't even exist yet.

The strategies we present here are a natural outgrowth of ideas about business that have gone before. They evolve the practice of innovation, design, and marketing in a direction demanded by the marketplace. We invite you to explore this concept with us. We hope you'll find it an enjoyable, thought-provoking read, offering perspective that just might revolutionize your business. At the very least, we think it will give you an opportunity and a vantage point from which to think about what your job means, and why that's an important consideration.

One

The Road to Meaning

In 1945, a young housewife walks to her local grocer every day. She brings a shopping list, but she doesn't need to be reminded to buy Pine-sol. Her mother always kept a bottle of the all-purpose household cleaner in her pantry, and now she does the same. Its pungent smell reassures her of its natural power to clean her house. Its concentrated formula helps her economize and stretch her budget a little further.

A generation later, in the 1970's, a young working mom stops at Kmart on her commute home. She races through the household cleaner aisle, grabbing a bottle of Formula 409 to clean her kitchen, Liquid Downy to soften her laundry, Lysol to disinfect her bathroom, and a new lemon-scented dishwashing liquid in case she needs it. These are the brands she recognizes, the ones she sees advertised on TV, the ones her friends use.

Three more decades pass and a single woman in her thirties waits for a connecting flight to visit her grandmother in Beijing. She has her laptop open and decides to check on a company she overheard a colleague raving about. She searches Google for "Method" and "soap." She reads a blog describing the idealistic entrepreneurial founders and the philosophy that shapes the company. She clicks on a link and a few seconds later smiles as the small company's website appears. This is it, she thinks, a company that seems to know her and offers a line of beautifully designed cleaning products that promise to love her home as much as she does.

People's needs and desires change over time. Sometimes companies are able to create supply in front of changing market demand, maybe even prompt it slightly. Sometimes businesses fall behind demand and must rush to catch up. Thousands of dissertations and countless consulting hours have been dedicated to figuring out the relationship between the forces of market supply and demand. It's an interesting topic and worthy of debate, but right now we're satisfied just knowing the two forces co-evolve. Our interest lies in anticipating the market's next move and ensuring that companies adopt innovation practices that are designed to respond quickly and appropriately to the change.

From our perspective, that change is happening now. It is a logical progression in the short history of consumer markets, and it revolves around people's growing appreciation of meaning in their lives—and their increasing expectation that companies can contribute to it. A brief review of innovation's path makes the emerging pattern clear and helps us see what's next.

From Mass to Niche

If we look back to the turn of the previous century—the late 1800's and early 1900's—we see inventive geniuses such as Thomas Edison, Henry Ford, and the team of William Procter and James Gamble innovating around two key factors: function and price. This was a very production-centric time, fueled by a "build it and they will come" philosophy that often worked. But as assembly lines and distribution infrastructure proliferated, companies developed more nuanced offerings beyond one-color autos and single-variety soaps. Given a choice, consumers similarly demanded these newly available attributes. As a result, innovation focused increasingly on iterations, extensions, and refinements of existing products. Soap manufacturers diversified into flakes, powders, and liquids. Food companies added new flavors. Catalogues grew larger. Invention and production still ruled the marketplace, but consumers' growing appetite for novelty and choice was a growing influence.

Evolution of innovation and consumer demand

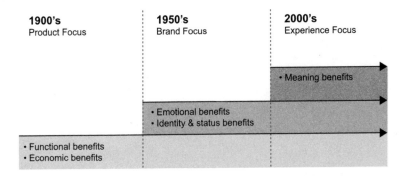

FIGURE 1: Evolution of innovation and consumer demand

In an effort to better understand consumers' beliefs and moti-
vations, a few pioneering organizations, including Cheskin, introduced the use of social science techniques in the 1930's and 1940's
to help companies and their ad agencies better understand why
people chose one product over another. These firms employed psy-
chologists, anthropologists, and sociologists who understood that
people's consumption patterns revealed a great deal about who
they were, how they viewed themselves, what they believed, and
how they lived. But at the time, companies were primarily interested in gaining greater persuasive powers and exerting more reliable control on consumer demand. They believed that decoding
human behavior would allow advertising and marketing not only
to raise product and brand awareness, but also to create and shape
consumer demand.

For a time, this worked. Throughout 1950's and 1960's, the
social research approach elevated the sophistication and effectiveness of marketing communication and helped create a mass consumer consciousness that responded almost instinctively to the
phrase "new and improved." Thanks to the emergence of broadcast
media and the popularity of daytime soap operas, a company could

invent a new toothpaste, detergent, or hairspray and confidently
predict its successful adoption based on a simple, research-derived
formula for gaining awareness, stimulating trial, and encouraging
repeat purchase. One 60-second commercial aired on a leading TV
soap opera could reach an audience of 30 million regular viewers
in the U.S., most of them women responsible for family purchases
who were also interested in buying what their neighbors bought.
Brand identity became one means by which new urbanites and
suburbanites were able to understand and communicate their place
in society during a period of rapid population expansion, increased
mobility, and new family formation.

During the tumult of the 1970's and early 1980's, the homogenous mass market began to disintegrate into a collection of niche
markets, characterized by progressively more confident consumers
who did not feel compelled to buy what everyone else bought. One
of the first segments to separate from the mass market were the
"Baby Boomers"—the youthful subgroup that had grown up watching TV commercials that defined the nation's buying habits. In
rebelling against their parents' tastes in clothing, cars, food, and
music, these young consumers brought explosive growth to companies like Levis, VW, Pepsi-Cola, Capitol Records, and McDonald's.
They convincingly demonstrated how companies and their products could thrive by focusing innovation on a particular market segment with distinct needs and desires.

As a result, innovation appropriately shifted from asking,
"How can we make everyone want this?" to "How can we make
what these people want?" The spotlight shifted from "features" to
"benefits." It was no longer enough to offer a functional product at
a fair price with a winning campaign. To succeed, a company had
to offer exactly the right product for the right reason, at the right
place, and at the right price. Marketing quickly embraced these four
"P's"—product, promotion, placement, and price—grabbing a

more commanding role in the innovation process and refocusing its persuasive power on smaller niches.

The break-up of the mass market and the resulting shift in innovation and marketing practices fueled a quantum leap in the number of new designs, unique feature sets, and brand identities— all vying for a small slice of the ever-growing consumer pie. Consumers developed a seemingly unquenchable thirst for "more" and "different," particularly if the product or service was a component of a branded "lifestyle" scenario. Coca-Cola went from offering a cola in one traditionally shaped bottle to offering a range of beverages in dozens of sizes and containers. General Motors introduced new brands every year, each intended for a more specific type of buyer. New magazines and newspapers popped up monthly, serving an ever more diverse constituency ranging from the recreational hunter to the teenage fashion lover. Ostensibly, no identified segment went unserved.

From Identity to Experience

It was during this period that the concept of branding seemed to go on steroids, pushing innovation beyond its focus on function and economic value to introducing new dimensions of identity and emotion. A generic credit card could distinguish itself by adopting the imagery of luxury and exclusivity, as American Express did. Pepsi could compete against an American classic like Coca-Cola by associating itself—and by extension, the person who drank Pepsi—with fun and popularity. As Louis Cheskin explained back then, "Choices are made emotionally much more frequently than rationally. The shopper is motivated by symbols, images, and colors." Today this concept seems so obvious as to be almost simplistic. We take it for granted that the Nike "swoosh" is a powerful symbol or that the richest coffee comes in brown packages. But throughout the latter decades of the 20th century, the brand identity concept was novel and fueled a mass remodeling of corporate logos, product packages, service uniforms, delivery trucks, and more.

Up to this point, we haven't talked specifically about the role of design in this evolutionary landscape. This is not an oversight. The role design plays here is difficult to map neatly onto this overview, in part because it is so broadly defined and applied, but also because design is so pervasive. For example, industrial designers often create devices, tools, and products that companies like Hewlett-Packard, Coleman, or GE sell. They also may specialize on shaping a product's physical form and style to improve the user's interaction with the product, and its overall appeal. Graphic designers use visual elements and text to communicate an idea, a concept, or a message. They also work with marketers to create packaging, advertising visuals, merchandising, product comps, and nearly everything else of a print nature. Information architects, another form of designer, structure information and data to make it more accessible. The newest entrants, digital designers, combine nearly everything that industrial, graphic, and information designers do. Much like architects (so much so that some hold the title of information architect), but working with digital, rather than tangible materials, they invent entire new types of businesses, like Amazon or eBay, complete with products, services, branding, distribution, consumer connections and, of course, pop-up ads. We haven't included interior designers, fashion designers, architects, or design engineers. As a category, designers' job responsibilities are simply too diverse to summarize, and it's impossible to assign them a singular role in the innovation process. Once form, identity, and emotion became significant factors in the ultimate success of a product, service, or brand, designers' influence began to concentrate and grow. Whatever the designer's specialty, he or she has a key role in seeing that the customer's experience of interacting with the product is a positive one.

By the end of the 20th century, the realm of innovation had expanded beyond inventors creating products and services to include marketers, who created brands, and designers who created and contributed a valuable but largely undefinable quality. In general, this widening notion of the innovation team contributed to greater levels of creativity and market relevance. But this convergence of professions, with their overlapping capabilities and passions, also fueled new tensions in many companies. It's easy to see why.

Who within a business has primary responsibility for directing innovation or for creating the next new thing: the inventors, the designers, or the marketers? If the responsibility is shared, who is in the lead role, and whose view of consumer's desires take precedence? This tension has been most evident at companies pursuing the creation of "experiences," a practice that rose out of the dotcom era encouraging companies to create products, services and environments based on a holistic consideration of the consumers' experience. We also find this debate about who directs innovation in companies that embrace 360 degree branding, a similar idea that says a company's brand communications should be consciously and consistently reinforced at all points of contact with its customers. Both approaches prioritize the customer, but both also blur the lines between the roles of inventor, designer, and marketer. These blurred lines can be the source of confusion and conflict within organizations. Should Microsoft's highly effective "realize your potential" marketing campaign control the design vision for Xbox? Was Gap's switch of its spokesperson from 40 year-old Sarah Jessica Parker to 18 year-old Joss Stone prompted by designers who needed to appeal to a younger generation market segment?

As a consequence of this tension between invention, design, and marketing, it has become common for us and other consulting firms to be contracted by a marketing executive who then directs us not to interact with the design or engineering department. Likewise, a design executive may contract us or other firms for an assignment and caution us not to let marketing know what they are doing. It's ironic, too, since to their credit, all sides espouse the value of deeply understanding their current and potential customers. Each has begun to respect the profound influence culture has on consumer perception and buying patterns. Each recognizes the importance of sharing customer understanding throughout organizations—in a manner that is accessible and inspiring, rather than relying on the mind-numbing charts and tables of past decades. And yet in many cases, these disciplines haven't learned to innovate collaboratively to truly achieve what their customers want. One side wins the battle, or everyone duplicates (even cancels out) each other's efforts.

Meanwhile the benefits of a designed experience start to be felt and enjoyed by consumers. The Starbucks coffee experience seems worth the higher price. Southwest's fun flying experience seems worth the inconvenience of no reserved seats. The cohesive, consistent quality of services like these heightens people's awareness and expectations of what companies should deliver. This growing expectation of an experience that integrates aspects of invention, design, and marketing, changes the stakes for the supply-side of the innovation equation. Now for a company to innovate effectively, these disciplines that used to function autonomously need to align and converge. All members of a company's innovation team need to work in unison to deliver a successful experience, particularly if that experience is to be meaningful.

The Demand for Meaning

The idea that companies can and should play a meaningful role in their customers' lives may sound grandiose to some, even dangerous to others, but it came to us quite simply and naturally. We didn't dream it up in a brainstorming session, or see it diagrammed by management gurus. We simply looked around and noticed people were talking more frequently and passionately about meaning in their lives. We heard people expressing a desire for—even expecting—meaningful experiences from companies, not just from traditional institutions such as religion, family, or government. As we mentioned earlier, we can't say for certain why this is happening, but we speculate that the demand for meaningful experiences is growing for several reasons.

In countries with advanced consumer markets where products and services are already designed to meet sophisticated emotional or identity needs, customers are seeking even more dimension. A teenage girl who has grown up with the Web, instant messaging, cell phones, and emoticons lights up when she learns about a new service that lets her and her friends develop a stronger sense of community by choosing, downloading, and listening to music together. She takes it for granted that her functional, economic, and emotional needs will be filled. Or as she might think of it, "It works, I can afford it, and it's cute." If a company offers something with more personal meaning to her—"It brings me and my friends together"—that's novel.

The U.S., Japan, and most European countries are all societies with an aging population. As people age they tend to have a broader perspective on the meaning of life and for many, an urgency to consider the meaning of life. It's much more common for us to hear a 50 year-old man talk about the meaningfulness of his travel experience than to have this same conversation with a 25 year-old. As people define what has meaning to them, they also define what is superficial to them. Older populations tend to have less time and less patience for the superficial.

In some countries, most notably the U.S., traditional sources of meaning have lost some their authority and as a result are not "producing" much meaning for people. Surveys of Americans' attitudes toward the press, the Supreme Court, the presidency, Congress, religious leaders, bosses, and other traditionally venerated authorities, have turned more negative compared to previous decades. Still, the desire for meaning is as old as humanity itself. It may even be the defining characteristic of what makes us human.

In any event, we believe addressing this emerging desire for meaning is innovation's newest evolutionary challenge, one that will require a highly collaborative development process and a focus on experience design. In the following chapters we explore the concept of meaning in the context of business, the design of meaningful customer experiences, and the specific processes that companies can use to innovate along these lines. We consider examples of companies that rethink and remodel their innovation processes to combine the skills of inventers, marketers, and designers. We describe companies that use consumer research at earlier points than is traditional and pursue techniques that provide them with deeper insights and understanding. We examine leading-edge firms that have realized that true value is determined by the customer's experience of their offerings—companies that believe as we do that the meaning of the customer experience is paramount.

> Twenty years from now, we will look back on the end of the 20th century and the beginning of the 21st as the starting point of a new kind of innovation in business, one that focuses its processes company-wide on the goal of providing its customers meaningful experiences.

If this idea still strikes some readers as outlandish or naïve, consider the Apple iPod. Perhaps no contemporary product provides a better illustration of what we're talking about. The iPod united Apple's product line, a related service (the iTunes Music Store), and a legion of third-party companies that scrambled to create peripherals and accessories. This wildly popular product integrated and reinforced a desirable musical experience. Advertising, promotion, product offerings, and a retail presence became a cohesive, unique, and highly entertaining customer experience. Yes, it was a clever invention, and yes, it was exceptionally well designed and marketed. But what makes the iPod an overwhelming success is the union of invention, design, and marketing into a seamless whole that evokes meaning in the enjoyment of music. By concentrating on the customer's experience, the iPod goes beyond simply selling devices, music, and peripherals to selling the sensation of freedom, control, wonder, beauty. Apple displayed genius connecting the iPod to meaning for its customers. But it's a process that others can, and should, follow.

It's our hope that 20 years from now, we will look back on the end of the 20th century and the beginning of the 21st as the starting point of a new kind of innovation in business, one that focuses its processes company-wide on the goal of providing its customers meaningful experiences.

Two

The Value of Meaning

Before going forward we must grapple with these two rather abstract terms: *experience and meaning.* Our brief recap in the previous chapter suggests that, at one level, the historical record of innovation is the story of companies progressively deepening their understanding of human needs and how their businesses can respond to those needs with goods and services. Over the course of the past century, this understanding progressed from meeting consumers' functional and economic requirements, through the emergence of choice and competition, culminating in the use of branding to address customers' desire for identity and, most recently, connections at the level of meaning. By mid-20th century, branding had become the essence of marketing and a defining characteristic of most global products and services. Brand was important to companies as a saleable asset; and it was important to customers as a distinction of value and identity.

Over the past few years, as branding and design evolved further, the term "experience" began to spread through businesses like the latest pop song. Executives would sing its refrains—experience marketing, holistic design, 360 degree branding, and so on—even if some didn't actually understand the lyrics. Whether instinctively or from feedback, they knew their customers sought both broader and deeper interactions with products and services than what could be represented on a feature list. These experiential relationships, they recognized, allowed them to create stronger ties between the company and its customers, and as such, generated more value to both.

The transition from a focus on brand identity to a focus on experience design was fueled in part by three influential business books. The first, *Experiential Marketing* by Bernd H. Schmitt, encouraged marketers to go beyond the limitations of traditional "features-and-benefits" marketing and move to a more holistic model of integrated, multisensory experiences. The second, *The Entertainment Economy,* by Michael Wolf, argued that all businesses will increasingly need to be entertaining to capture and hold customers' interest. The third book, *The Experience Economy,* by Joseph Pine and James H. Gilmore, articulated the idea that, "When a person buys a service, he purchases a set of intangible activities carried out on his behalf. But when he buys an experience, he pays to spend time enjoying a series of memorable events that a company stages—as in a theatrical play—to engage him in a personal way." These authors' vision resonated widely with product and service developers who began to introduce the idea of using the customer experience as a framework for tactical design and development. Similarly inspired, brand strategists, marketers, and designers also began to apply the concept to broaden the dimension of advertising and other forms of communication.

Experience Defined

Regardless of what we call it, an "experience" can be described simply as the sensation of change. In other words, an experience is any process we're conscious of and involved in as it happens. To experience something requires that we recognize an alteration to our environment, our bodies, our minds, our spirits, or any other aspect of ourselves that can sense change. We all have experiences every day ranging from the superficial to the profound. Some experiences are simple, like drinking a glass of water on a hot day to physically cool down. Others incorporate ritual or tap into wider associations, such as chugging an ice-cold beer in a neighborhood bar after a blistering day of hard work, recalling past sensations of relaxation or fun. Some experiences are logical reactions, for example, watching a documentary that presents a perspective so convincingly and in such detail that we are are aware of being enlightened on the topic, perhaps even persuaded to change our view about it. Others are more emotional or visceral, like sitting through a movie that lifts our mood, or one that makes us hide our eyes and physically cringe. Still other experiences are manufactured for a mass market and delivered through designed artifacts, like the environments of Disneyland and Las Vegas, the sound of a Harley-Davidson, or the "white space" of Google. And some, like hugging your child or feeling a breeze at the beach, are natural, impulsive, and always changing.

From a marketing and design perspective, an experience is an engagement delivered to the customer through an integrated system of "touch points"—product, packaging, message, customer service, and so on—that conveys or evokes a consistent sense of its essence. The goal of experience branding or experience design is admirable: it reflects a company's effort to be consistent in its value proposition and its expression in every connection with a consumer. When practiced to its fullest, these experiences are delivered not only through a company's product or service, but also through its choice of distribution channel, how it advertises, how it merchandises, where its products are manufactured, how it trains employees, and even through its choice of CEO.

One recent example of a company embracing the idea of experience design is Procter & Gamble, a bellwether company for management practices. With a practical, conservative Midwestern culture, this global corporation researches and experiments with new approaches but generally resists trends until their contribution to performance is clear. Leveraging deep customer understanding, its innovation process now seeks to integrate brand, advertising, packaging, and product design by coordinating all touch points using customer experience as its focal point. As Procter & Gamble's CEO, A.G. Lafley told *Fast Company* magazine in a June 2005 interview, "We want to design the purchasing experience—what we call the 'first moment of truth'—we want to design every component of the product; and we want to design the communication experience and the user experience."

This type of commitment is impressive, and we applaud those companies like P&G that are pursuing the intentional design of experiences. But seeking to turn every consumer interaction into an experience, no matter how consistent and engaging, has a couple of serious flaws: First, it's simply not possible for a company to consciously design every touch point with a customer. Pepsi works diligently to control the use of its logo, but it still turns up on black market T-shirts revised to suit a caption or to make a subversive point, such as a recent version we found where the name "Pepsi" was replaced in the logo with "Penis." Most people of course recognize that the shirt with the altered logo doesn't come from Pepsi, but it still makes a logo impression. Wells Fargo designs a consistent message of its value to customers that is conveys through its advertising and merchandising, but it can't completely control what is said about its services through word of mouth.

Apart from the impossibility of completely controlling all touch points in an experience, there's positive value in intentionally relinquishing some control and encouraging customers to participate in co-creating experiences. That process itself deepens the individual customer's connection to the product and company. Part of the global appeal of Starbucks is the satisfaction each customer gets from personalizing her beverage each time she visits, even if her preference means the barista will be making a weak cup of coffee that Starbucks would never endorse. Cold Stone Creamery pursues this same goal in letting each customer customize his ice cream by mixing in as many candies, flavors, and ingredients as he likes. Websites like Yahoo! and MSN encourage customers to design their own start pages based on their preferences, and digital TV recorders like TiVo allow a viewer to customize his selection of programs, while skipping any parts he doesn't like.

Another flaw in the current approach to designing experiences is the failure to distinguish between significant impressions and trivial ones. While it may be appropriate and entertaining for a theme restaurant to dress its staff in costumes and interrupt lunch every ten minutes with a singing waiter, this type of experience doesn't translate well to banking. The loud, fast, and irreverent antics of MTV events and programming appeal to its fans, but that doesn't mean it's an experience even they want from a hospital.

Companies miss the point if they think of experiences simply in terms of multisensory expressions of brand, looping in previously underserved senses like sound, and touch. An experience can be created by designing all potential touch points, surrounding the customer with a highly coordinated environment wherever she turns, but it takes something more to make these experiences valuable so that customers connect personally with them and integrate them into their lives. We think that "something" is meaning.

The Meaning of Meaning

We first became aware of this role of meaning when we interviewed people about their lives and found that there were certain products and services that were as tightly integrated into their daily reality as family and friends. A South Carolina man talked about his relationship with Coca-Cola in the same way he talked about his wife, describing how he and his favorite carbonated beverage had grown up together, were shaped by the same historical events, went to the same parties, and had both settled into a comfortable "middle age." We talked with a fashionable woman who described how she and Victoria's Secret were working together to find her a mate. A young

Latina confided that Josephina, her American Girl doll, was her "best friend" and that they faced the same challenges in school. These were not conversations about "values-based" marketing, where people were buying or boycotting to express a shared point of view. Instead, we found something even more fundamental. We found that people had the strongest ties to products, services and brands that evoked meaningful experiences for them.

The definition of meaning that underlies the ideas we're putting forth is that of connotation, worth, or import, as in "This place has meaning to me," or in a slightly different form, "Our 4th of July parade is always a meaningful event." Unfortunately, this is the often the most vague and subjective of meaning's definitions. If someone says her hometown has meaning or that he had a meaningful experience at a parade, she could be indicating patriotic sensibilities, dysfunctional influences, emotional ties, status associations, personal identification, and a host of other attributes. There's no way to really understand what she is telling us until we collect a few more adjectives. Once these experiences are characterized a little more descriptively, however, we can learn a great deal about them. If someone honestly shares with us the meanings in his life as he interprets it, we can anticipate much about his desires and behavior.

If someone tells us, "This place has meaning to me because it unites me with a community," we know she will prefer a home where she identifies with her neighbors, where the community's values and related behaviors are understood and supported and where her standard of living is on par with her peers.

If someone tells us, "This place has meaning to me because it gives me a sense of accomplishment," it's likely this person will look for a home that reflects his economic or social achievements, where he will be distinguished from others and where his standard of living may be higher than those around his.

If someone tells us, "This place has meaning to me because it feeds my sense of wonder and awe," we know something about his need to live in an environment that allows significant exploration and experimentation, where he can move at his own pace and where standard of living may be irrelevant.

Shared Meaning

In his 1977 seminal work, *The Interpretation of Culture,* Clifford Geertz, one of the preeminent thinkers in contemporary anthropology, noted that meaning doesn't just emerge from our genes, or from our Creator, complete and ready for use. Instead, Geertz explained, meaning is our mind's construction of reality, the translation of existence into conceptual form. Why do we construct meaning in the first place? Aside from reflexes and instincts, human beings require an explanation of the world that helps us decide how to act. Meaning helps us understand the world and ourselves, learn, and make sense of what's around us. It provides a framework for assessing what we value, believe, condone, and desire. Anything that supports a sense of meaning supports the basis for understanding and action, making it extremely valuable to us.

In the last few decades, the anthropological view of meaning has been joined by a new, biological approach in the discipline of cognitive neuroscience, a branch of biological psychology that focuses on the neural mechanisms by which we learn. Its leading practitioners have concluded that the human brain's capacity to construct meaning has evolved over many millennia. Once cultural forms began (things like language, images, artifacts, and organizations), those people who could work with them at ever more complex levels possessed a survival advantage over those who couldn't. Consequently, those of us currently living on the planet have become experts at constructing meaning because it enhances our ability to survive in a world of meanings. In the modern human, the ability—and the need—to construct meaning are at the heart of what makes us human. In short, both the anthropologists and neuroscientists agree that meaning is the sense we make of reality, and this is the definition we adhere to. Assigning meaning to experience is how each of us creates the story of our life and its ultimate value and purpose.

As this definition suggests, and hosts of anthropologists and historians attest, the impulse to translate experience into meaning has been with us since the beginning of civilization. In early societies, small groups of people collectively constructed forms and symbols which conveyed a shared sense of meaning. Language—both speech and gesture—was probably the first vehicle for transmitting shared meaning, but objects would have quickly followed. Artifacts like bowls, special articles of clothing, and weapons were often believed to embody meaning, and even to bring meaning into the world.

These early constructions of shared meaning had significant power to shape and control people's lives. They evolved into religions, forms of government, status systems, and mass movements. Cultural systems of meaning remained stable over long periods of time, controlled in many cases by just a few institutions, such as the church, family, and governing bodies. Ceremonies and rituals reinforced the most centrally valued concepts in a society and were a means of carrying them from generation to generation. Throughout most of human history, baptisms, coming of age rites, weddings, and wakes have all been systems of transmitting meaning, as have more contemporary rituals such as initiations, swearing-in ceremonies, graduations, and numerous other occasions for pomp and circumstance. With time, their origins may have been lost to most practitioners, but these meaningful experiences nevertheless continue to influence us and shape our lives.

Personal Meaning

As we've moved from caves and tribes into condos and workgroups, meaning in life has become less about what commonly held traditions demand of us and reinforce in us, and more about what we choose for ourselves. Traditional kinship and social class distinctions break down and reconfigure cultural systems and other structures for defining and controlling meaning in society. Exposure to new societies expands our definition of what's acceptable, what's normal, and what's significant. Scientific discoveries and the spread of education present alternative views of reality and encourage the active challenging of what were previously undisputed meaning. And most recently, the advancement of technology has given people both the tools to customize meaning in their lives and greater information to influence it. In other words, one of the reasons we collectively need dozens of different lattes, hundreds of car models, thousands of loan programs, and millions of downloadable songs is not just because we're fickle consumers. It's because each of these items is a building block in the reality we construct for ourselves, and as such, we increasingly prefer they fit our concept of self. This is what we mean by meaningful consumption. As we selectively purchase or reject these items, they become inextricably part of how we construct meaning in our lives.

Those of us watching the evolution of the U.S. mass market have seen this evolution from shared to personal meaning unfold in an almost orchestrated way. In the 1950's and 1960's Americans bought Wonder Bread, Campbell's Soup, and Chevy station wagons, largely because everyone else did but also because it signified our shared values and what we collectively believed was meaningful in life. When we later fragmented into market segments, we still held consumer beliefs in common and shared constructions of meaning expressed by the products and services we bought, but within smaller groups, typically aligned with a particular lifestyle. We became suburbanites who bought Weber barbecues because entertaining was meaningful us, or Yuppies who drove BMWs because accomplishment was meaningful to us, or sporty teenager who wore Nikes because performance was meaningful to us. Rather than remaining an homogenous group waiting to learn what new benefit we should value or what new invention we should buy en masse, consumers diverged first into niche markets and most recently into micro-markets—in some cases, markets of one.

For many consumers, being associated with a group and following the group's lead is comforting, stabilizing, and reassuring. In fact, some people derive a sense of meaning and security from being like selected others equivalent to what others derive from religion or family. But increasingly, particularly among teens and young adults who were raised with the influence of global communities and the World Wide Web, we find people for whom it makes no sense to simply accept traditional lifestyle definitions without exploring the extensive alternatives. Why build your life like your parents, your neighbors, or your friends when you have the tools, the options, and the information to design something that's a perfect fit for you? This attitude, which says, "I am responsible for creating the reality of my life," brings with it a more discerning consumerism. All the previous attributes of products, services, and brands may still be important. We may still want economic value, status, identity, and emotional ties, but we want them within an overall meaning or set of meanings that are exactly right for us.

Corporate Meaning

Whether we align ourselves with others or instead seek uniqueness, products, services, and experiences have value in that they add meaning to some part of our story. If we think of meaning as something people use to construct and make sense of their lives, we can see how all the objects, interactions, and environments we experience throughout the day become intertwined to make up an ongoing narrative. We may think of daily habits as fixed behaviors we've adopted over time, but we can also think of them as the repetition of certain parts of our life story. We may spontaneously try something new and describe that as impulse, but it's also an attempt to interject a new scene or character in our personal story—a deeper, more significant reality—while sticking with the overall plot line of our lives.

As business people trained to focus on the financial value of goods and services, it may be difficult to accept the bottom-line value of reshaping our innovation processes around the expression of meaning. We've traditionally judged a company's success by its profitability, its investment potential, its sales growth, or its financial equity. More recently we've begun to include customer satisfaction, customer retention, brand equity, and other less tangible assets in the mix, and a few companies are even beginning to include the effects their decisions have on society and the environment. With the exception of social and environmental effects, these are all fairly quantifiable metrics tied to processes and standards. They are well understood and widely accepted. While we may understand that meaning in life matters, we're more likely to think about it in church, or while we watch our children play. Meaning is a part of our personal life, and many of us assume it can't really impact business value beyond having a meaningful job or a meaningful relationship with co-workers. In fact, some may even consider it an inappropriate focus of business that blurs the line between commerce and philosophy or rational transactions and spiritual values.

But businesses are already crossing that line. Although most have avoided stepping directly into the meaning market with their offerings, they have aggressively done so with their PR. During breaks on Sunday morning talk shows, commercials from sponsors like General Electric, CIT, BP, and Archer Daniels Midland frequently go beyond highlighting products or services and instead promote a more transcendent meaning of their business. Archer Daniels Midland, one of the world's largest agricultural processors, is also "creating a world of possibilities from a single seed." BP, a global energy company, "contributes to a better quality of life," and at its core has "an unshakable commitment to human progress." We might be tempted to dismiss these taglines as simply evidence of creative spin to counter complaints about their size, their power, or their business practices, but they suggest that these companies wish to convey a belief in more than next quarter's profits.

A few companies go beyond corporate posturing and mission statements and already convey a sense of meaning to their customers through their products and positioning. Companies like Harley-Davidson, Coca-Cola, Apple, and Budweiser may not define themselves explicitly by the meaning they provide their customers, but many of their customers nonetheless find meaning in their brands and happily integrate that meaning into their lives. While these companies may not have consciously coordinated all aspects of a consumer experience or specifically designed the types of meaning they evoke, their product features, names, logos, industrial design, color schemes, and imagery create cohesive themes that resonate with people. As a result, each has a thriving business selling apparel, memorabilia and other items that people happily buy as reminders of meaning, much as earlier generations bought saints or relics. In contrast, although companies like Citibank and Intel are undeniably successful from a financial point of view, we rarely if ever meet people who put the Intel logo on their bedroom walls or proudly wear a Citibank T-shirt to a concert. They may like these companies and use their products and services, but there's rarely a meaningful connection in the relationship.

When a company can evoke meaning through its products or services, it is tapping in to what people value most in life. We bond with products, services, and brands based on our "experience" of them and how they evoke meaning to us. The companies that recognize the importance of these experiences and provide them to us become the co-creators of our lives. This type of bond between a company and a consumer goes beyond customer satisfaction and brand building. Rather than being a component of marketing or design, designing experiences that evoke meaning is the heart and soul of innovation. As companies look to please customers not as something secondary to growth that lives in the marketing department but as the basis for growth itself, innovation is fueled and directed in a way that creates competitive advantage and lasting competitive advantage for the corporation.

Three

A World of Meaningful Experiences

Humans have evolved to value increasingly complex meaning in their lives, an evolution that is partly reflected in our consumption of goods and services. This evolution has proceeded from a primary focus on function and economic value to the addition of progressively more intricate offerings like status and emotional value, and now meaning. Worldwide, consumers are increasingly seeking products and services that connect with them through meaning, that jive with their sense of how the world is, or should be. Although this trend is prevalent in the West, we see increasing evidence of it globally. Just as tribes, traditions, and objects brought order and "rightness" to people in previous centuries, a company and its offerings may now play that role as well by solidifying a relationship at the deepest possible point in the human psyche and personality. It's a potent place for a company to be.

Companies have been both lauded and derided in the past for creating lifestyles, particularly consumer lifestyles. We're not convinced they've actually done so. Instead, we think companies have become adept at making a connection from products and services to emerging lifestyles and trends. They may have embraced these new directions, and perhaps amplified them, but not actually created them. Similarly, we're not arguing that companies are in a position to create meaning in people's lives, rather that they are in a position to connect to meanings people already recognize and want.

Companies can address people's growing desire for meaning by intentionally designing cohesive experiences based on a specific meaning and expressed cohesively through products, services, and other consumer touch points.

Experiences with Global Appeal

What types of meaningful experiences do people value? In the course of helping companies develop products and services that suit their markets, every year we interview over 100,000 individuals from countries and cultures around the world. In these interviews, we've found commonalities among the meanings people feel strongly about, whether we're studying the adoption of new software in Poland or the purchase of toothbrushes in Florida.

We've compiled a list of these meanings, but it is far from exhaustive. We've found potentially dozens of types of meaningful experiences and at least as many possible ways to characterize them. What we concentrate on here are 15 of the meanings that emerge most frequently in these interviews and appear to be universal among people's values. While the relative importance of these meaningful experiences might vary and their interpretation could differ slightly, all cultures seem to recognize their significance. This is good news for businesses, because it means that there is a certain constancy among human needs that transcends the distinctions of culture and language.

(Since none of these meaningful experiences is more or less important than any other, we've presented them in alphabetical order.)

1. Accomplishment—Achieving goals and making something of oneself; a sense of satisfaction that can result from productivity, focus, talent, or status. American Express has long benefited from transmitting a hint of this meaning to its card holders by establishing itself as a credit card intended for those who are successful. Nike relies on the essence of this meaning for many in its "Just Do It" campaign.

2. Beauty—The appreciation of qualities that give pleasure to the senses or spirit. Of course beauty is in the eye of the beholder and thus highly subjective, but our desire for it is ubiquitous. We aspire to beauty in all that surrounds us, from architecture and fine furnishing to clothing and cars. Enormous industries thrive on the promise of beauty stemming from shinier hair, whiter teeth, and clearer skin. Beauty can also be more than mere appearance. For some, it is a sense that something is created "correctly" or efficiently with an elegance of purpose and use. Companies such as Bang & Olufsen audio equipment and Jaguar automobiles distinguish themselves through the beauty of their design.

3. Creation—The sense of having produced something new and original, and in so doing, to have made a lasting contribution. Besides driving our species to propagate, we enjoy this experience through our hobbies, the way we decorate our home, in telling our stories, and in anything else that reflects our personal choices. Creation is what makes "customizable" seem like a desirable attribute, rather than more work for the buyer, for example, making the salad bar a pleasure rather than a chore.

4. Community—A sense of unity with others around us and a general connection with other human beings. Religious communities, unions, fraternities, clubs, and sewing circles are all expressions of a desire for belonging. The promise and delivery of community underlies the offerings of several successful organizations including NASCAR with its centralizing focus on car racing and leagues of loyal fans that follow the race circuit, Harley-Davidson motorcycles and their Harley Owners Group (HOG), and Jimmy Buffet with his dedicated Parrotheads. These businesses attract and support user communities who embody specific values tied to their products and services.

5. Duty—The willing application of oneself to a responsibility. The military in any country counts on the power of this meaning, as do most employers. Duty can also relate to responsibilities to oneself or family, such as reading the daily paper to stay abreast of the news. Commercially, anything regarded as "good for you," including vitamins, medications, Cross-Your-Heart bras, and cushioned insoles relays some sense of duty and the satisfaction it brings.

6. Enlightenment—Clear understanding through logic or inspiration. This experience is not limited to those who meditate and fast, it is a core expectation of offerings from Fox News, which promises "fair and balanced" reporting, the *Wall Street Journal*, which many consider the ultimate authority for business news, and the Sierra Club, which provides perspective on environmental threats and conservation.

7. Freedom—The sense of living without unwanted constraints. This experience often plays tug-of-war with the desire for security; more of one tends to decrease the other. Nevertheless, freedom is enticing, whether it's freedom from dictators, or in the case of Google, the freedom to quickly search the Web learning and interacting with millions of people and resources.

8. Harmony—The balanced and pleasing relationship of parts to a whole, whether in nature, society, or an individual. When we seek a work/life balance, we are in pursuit of harmony. Likewise, when we shop at Target for a toaster that matches our mixer, we are in pursuit of harmony. Much of the aesthetic appeal of design depends on our personal desire for the visual experience of harmony.

9. Justice—The assurance of equitable and unbiased treatment. This is the sense of fairness and equality that underlies our concept of "everyman" or Average Joe. It helps explain the immense popularity of the Taurus and the Camry, the ranch house, Levi's jeans, and white cotton T-shirts—all products with a simple, impartial appeal to a very broad audience.

10. Oneness—A sense of unity with everything around us. It is what some seek from the practice of spirituality and what others expect from a good tequila. Although we don't normally think of them as a company, the Grateful Dead sustained its revenues for decades building an experience that connected with its fans' desire for oneness. Similarly, organizations that connects their members into nature or a broader sense of the world, like the Monterey Bay Aquarium or the United Nations, are capable of evoking a meaning of oneness.

11. Redemption—Atonement or deliverance from past failure or decline. Though this might seem to stem from negative experiences, the impact of the redemptive experience is highly positive. Like community and enlightenment, redemption has a basis in religion, but it also attracts customers to Weight Watchers, Bliss spas, and the grocery store candy aisle. Any sensation that delivers us from a less desirable condition to a more pleasing another one can be redemptive.

12. Security—The freedom from worry about loss. This experience has been a cornerstone of civilization but in the U.S. in particular, acquired increased meaning and relevance after 9/11. On the commercial side, the desire for this experience created the insurance business, and it continues to sell a wide range of products from automatic rifles to Depends undergarments to credit cards that offer protection from identity theft.

13. Truth—A commitment to honesty and integrity. This experience plays an important role in most personal relationships, but it also is a key component of companies like Whole Foods, Volkswagen, and Newman's Own, all of which portray themselves as simple, upright, and candid.

14. Validation— The recognition of oneself as a valued individual worthy of respect. Every externally branded piece of clothing counts on the attraction of this meaningful experience whether it's Ralph Lauren Polo or Old Navy, as does Mercedes-Benz, the Four

Seasons hotel chain, and any other brand with status identification as a core value.

15. Wonder—Awe in the presence of a creation beyond one's understanding. While this might sound mystical and unattainable, consider the wonder that Las Vegas hotels create simply through plaster and lights. Disney has been a master of this experience for decades, and technology companies routinely evoke awe as they enable their users to do what seemed impossible the year before.

But What About...?

At the end of any list, someone is sure to ask about what's missing. Why don't we include "control," "enrichment," or "happiness" on this list? Rather than defend this particular set of meaningful experiences, we recommend that you use these as a starting points for considering the meaningful experiences your own company, products, services, or related offerings might evoke. Depending on the category and audience, other meaningful experiences could be just as effective as long as they represent what your customers deeply value (not what the company wants them to value). For example, "happiness" or "satisfaction" is nearly always the result of one of the experiences on our list, rather than an end in and of itself. "Enrichment" is often what a company thinks it provides for a consumer's life, but it is not a meaning the consumer seeks.

Readers prone to nuance might look at the list and say, "These are not meanings but rather values." We believe there is an important distinction to be made between values and meaning. Values involve preferences. They represent our choices between opposing modes of behavior, and they are shaped not only by ourselves, but also by those around us. For example, I may prefer being a vegetarian because I believe it's the best mode of eating for my health or because I'm an advocate of animal rights. In this belief, I'm expressing a value. But practicing vegetarianism ultimately serves my sense of oneness, community, and maybe truth. That's meaning.

Is it really possible to create the meaningful experience of security or harmony for someone, or does a person need to create it for himself? This is a legitimate concern and one worth exploring more fully. As we've suggested, the experience people have with products, services, and events is only partly due to what a company might envision and endeavor to provide. The bulk of the experience is actually created by the experiencer; that's how it becomes highly relevant for the individual. A company could never create exactly the meaningful experience a consumer wanted because companies can't completely understand every detail of each person's life, and it can't control every interaction of the experience. However, a company can learn enough about its customers to design an experience for them that conveys its intention and prompts them to complete it. This is why we say companies *evoke* meaning through experiences, rather than creating meaning.

Turning the Ordinary into the Meaningful

If all this seems at times to verge on the theoretical, we'll demonstrate how meaningful experiences can transform products and services. Unfortunately, at this point in our history, there aren't many companies doing this well or consciously, so examples beyond the partial expressions from companies cited in the list above are limited.

One of the best examples is Method, a small company that decided to use this approach to challenge some of the world's most dominant and entrenched competitors in its category. Method operates in a category that fairly screams "functional"—household cleaning supplies, which is dominated by massive global companies including Procter & Gamble, Unilever, and Clorox.

Until Method appeared on the scene, household cleaning products could be defined by their glaring colors, generic shapes, large containers, and chemical smells. A blind person could easily find the cleaning aisle in any store just by following the harsh scent of disinfectants, deodorizers, and powerful cleaning agents. Anyone who introduced a "kinder, gentler" approach to cleaning was immediately relegated to the aisle reserved for poor-selling "green" products. To compete in this category, you had to be a germ-killing, grease-dissolving giant.

But Method thought differently. Co-founders Eric Ryan and Adam Lowry started by taking an ordinary experience—cleaning the house—and making it more meaningful. As Ryan says, "Our goal was to make chores less of a chore. We thought we could do this by creating experiences that expressed our consumers' love for their home and tying that to our products. If people don't have to look at cleaning as killing germs, but as doing something positive for their home, the power of the experience goes deeper than the activity. It's touching something primal."

With this grounding, Ryan and Lowry went on to invent a company they describe as "people against dirty." But their definition of "dirty" includes not just germs and grime, but also toxic chemicals, non-recyclable packaging material, and destructive production practices. They promote their products as "a cleaner way of cleaning," and each is highly effective, environmentally safe, and packaged to be physically beautiful enough to be left on a counter after it's used. Even Method's advertising is part of the experience. As Ryan explains, "Our 'People Get Dirty' campaign talks about the experience of cleaning, not the products. The number of customer emails we've received in response is groundbreaking. Customers say they are finally excited about cleaning. These products were things they dreaded buying, and now they have turned into something they *want* to buy."

Nice concept, but is Method successful? After only six years, Method is actually giving those giant global companies reason to be nervous. Why? Because Method's products are now sold in Costco, Target, and most recently Wal-Mart. And they sell fast.

Like their competitors, Method's cleaning products function well. Its advertising provides effective emotional ties and, to some consumers, its brand conveys status. It does what everyone else in the category does, but it provides these attributes within a context of meaning that connects with its consumers. By supporting its customers' desire for an experience of oneness and harmony, it has transformed cleaning from drudgery to a joy and overcome the perception that environmentally sound household cleaners are too weak to be effective.

Another company that benefits from connecting with its customers in a surprisingly meaningful way is Bush Beans. This mid-sized, family-owned company produces and sells a wide range of canned beans. It would be difficult to find a simpler category, and as a result, most rivals compete on price. But Bush succeeds with a different recipe—by offering the consumer the experience of connecting with family—the Bush family, to be exact. The company owners (even the family dog) are important brand assets, populating the website, starring in the ads, writing the newsletter, and generally embodying the company's emphasis on community and truth. Their beans evoke a sense of family life, and that intangible value keeps their line of beans and chili on the store shelf next to those offered by giants ConAgra, Del Monte, and Kraft.

Like Method, Bush Beans offers consumers the same function and economic value as its competitors offer, but by conveying them within the context of a meaningful experience—that of love for one's family and connectedness—the company is able to make a deeper connection with its customers.

In showcasing these two smaller companies that successfully compete against larger ones, we don't mean to imply that this approach doesn't work for larger companies. Quite the contrary. In fact, throughout this book you'll find references to large companies such as Apple Computer, Starbucks, Southwest Airlines, and others that are delivering some level of meaningful experiences to their customers. There is ample opportunity for large companies to reinvigorate their consumer connections by adopting this philosophy, as the example of OnStar demonstrates. When GM bought Hughes Aircraft Company in 1985, it seemed like an odd pairing of two different product categories with unrelated functionality. Ten years later, GM used the satellite capabilities from its Hughes acquisition in partnership with systems developer EDS to create OnStar, which it marketed as a GPS feature providing directional assistance to drivers of upscale cars. Soon after its introduction, OnStar highlighted its ability to provide "remote diagnostics" on engine performance, and then tried a concierge service that offered to help drivers buy flowers and find restaurants. It evolved again, teaming with media like Disney, Dow Jones, and ESPN to see if entertainment or information was an offering subscribers' valued. Unfortunately, all of these additions were just various functional benefits, valued differently depending on the subscriber. When OnStar really started to connect with consumers is when it repositioned itself as synonymous with "security," providing help "out of the blue" whenever a driver needed it. By aligning all its capabilities with a recognized and coveted meaning, the combination of satellites and cars finally made sense to a much larger audience.

Other large companies could follow suit. Thanks to its heritage and reputation for quality, Sears could convincingly deliver on wisdom, truth, and maybe even community by rethinking its role in a neighborhood or what common value unites it many products and services. Could SBC Communications evoke enlightenment or freedom by unifying and elevating the diverse functional benefits of phone service and DSL connections? Could Hewlett-Packard really deliver a sense of creation beyond its clever "Invent" campaign if its products and services were less associated with productivity and work?

Any company can take an ordinary experience that offers functional, economic, or emotional values and increase the significance level to that of meaning. However, it usually requires reversing the order of its traditional development process to start with understanding customers rather than an understanding of materials, functions or identity. In the next several chapters, we'll go into the details of doing this successfully.

Four

Finding a Starting Point

Companies don't just wake up one morning and decide to start making meaningful experiences for their customers. Like people, companies develop habits and patterns that are difficult to change, and the commitment to meaningful experiences requires full company support. To be successful, a company needs to integrate meaning throughout its development process and in every area of innovation, starting from the identification of opportunity and proceeding all the way through maintaining customer relationships. Making meaning is a company-wide initiative.

For that reason, a good starting point for a company that wants to build meaningful experiences for its customers is to assess what type of innovation culture it currently has. While this may seem like a "cart before the horse" activity, we've found that setting the context and establishing a workable plan greatly facilitates and improves a company's ability to both understand people's desires for meaning and respond appropriately to them.

Defining Your Company's Innovation Culture

For some readers, it might seem as if your company hasn't innovated anything for the last 20 years (except perhaps in its creative avoidance of change). For others, your company might engage in relentless change. Regardless, every company has an innovation culture that drives its rate of change and controls its innovation process. While

Which type of innovation culture does your company have?

Experience Innovation Culture	Creative Innovation Culture	Dynamic Innovation Culture
• Innovation is the outcome of a formal process	• "Big Ideas" inspire most innovation initiatives	• Strategic thinking guides overall process
• Leadership by middle management, R&D, and technology departments	• Led by senior management	• Led by senior management with cross-functional teams
• Cross-functional collaboration is not emphasized	• Execution is often ad hoc and doesn't follow a set process	• Cross-functional collaboration is important
• Analytic evaluations are usually more important than creativity	• Curiosity and creativity are more important than analytics	• A creative environment is important, but innovation is not dependent on the "big idea"
• Most innovations are iterative and risk is minimized	• Risk taking is accepted	• Risk taking is accepted

FIGURE 4.1: What is your company's culture of innovation? See which description best fits your company's current approach.

innovation cultures can be changed, it's usually much easier and more productive to work within the system that's already in place.

Cheskin recently undertook a study to see how companies across the U.S. approach innovation. We found that most companies currently innovate in one of three distinct methods: structured, creative, or dynamic. The structured approach to innovation, used by roughly 18 percent of companies studied, is an outgrowth of the industrial era and follows a strict and formalized process engineered to be efficient and replicable. This approach depends more heavily on internal leadership, strategic planning, effective execution, shareholder pressure, and financial resources than do other approaches. Structured innovation places less weight on a creative environment, the value of curiosity, or risk taking. Usually, a firm with this type of approach in place has a policy governing how innovation is practiced and a department devoted to that goal. This might sound like an approach that could only live in an enormous corporation, but in fact it is as popular among medium-sized organizations (100 to 999 employees) as it is among larger ones. In these environments, management of the innovation process is typically delegated to more junior executives and is often the sole province of product management or R&D.

More common (26 percent) are companies that use an informal and creative innovation process that depends heavily on the "big idea." To these companies, predominantly small firms, innovation is less likely to be a structured process led by strategic thinking and planning and more likely to be based on inspiration. The owner may announce in a meeting that he has a "great idea" and assign some people to begin developing it. Unlike those in the structured-process camp, these companies tend not to worry much about execution because responsibility for innovation generally remains within a small group of executive managers or a creative team. In these environments, supporting a creative culture, taking risks, and exercising curiosity all outweigh risk analysis and financial considerations.

The largest percentage of companies we studied (39 percent) exhibit a dynamic innovation process that combines flexibility and creativity with some structure. This approach favors strategic thinking and planning along with a respect for execution, but it also depends on cross-functional collaboration and keeps senior executives actively engaged. The process emphasizes a creative culture but values the importance of having a pipeline of innovation, rather than betting on singular ideas. The perception of risk within these companies is based on a realistic acknowledgment of the many conditions that can thwart their efforts, including funding, time-to-market pressure, gaining internal buy-in, and consumer acceptance. In these firms, which range from small to large, employees across many departments help the company find opportunities, create new ideas, and bring them to fruition. Ideally this process is coordinated, but it can easily become chaotic.

While we believe the dynamic approach to innovation is most efficient and effective, any of these three approaches can incorporate and support the design of meaningful experiences—if the right team is driving its adoption and execution.

Structuring Change

The team for creating meaningful experiences should not consist solely of any one profession but should integrate representation of the company's designers, researchers, developers, marketers, and senior executives at a minimum. The right team represents each of these functions and synchronizes their collaboration toward a shared outcome. Rather than one department or function "owning" innovation, the *team* owns the overall design vision and ensures that its delivery is consistently coordinated across the company. For example, if a company is planning to introduce a new athletic shoe, the innovation team creates not only the vision of the new shoe but also the plan for how every department in the company will help create, execute and support that vision. This ability to foster cross-boundary collaboration and to recognize that every major department has a role to play is critical to designing meaningful experiences because it heightens the likelihood that all customer touch points of the experience will be cohesive and consistent. Pursuing this type of collaboration also helps ensure more internal buy-in of the process and its results, typically accelerating development and increasing the intensity of everyone's participation.

Of course, this is more easily said than done. A common pitfall is the omission of an important team member. For example, a major consumer electronics company recently embarked on a global redesign program to express meaning through its brands and products. While the program was very successful at many levels, it failed to achieve its real potential because the innovation team excluded the user interface group. The team developed attractive hardware and a motivating brand experience, but customers' interactions with the product were inconsistent with its appearance and identity. From the customer's perspective, the actual experience of using the device was incomplete and disjointed. This unsatisfying experience with the interface overshadowed the positive attributes of the device and the brand and decreased its appeal.

The ideal composition of your company's innovation team will vary depending on whether your focus is on incremental or breakthrough innovation. Incremental innovation tends to depend more on the process focus of middle management, while breakthrough innovation usually requires the commitment and authority of senior management. As a general rule of thumb, however, any significant customer touch point should be represented on the innovation team. For example, if the bulk of a company's new sales are expected to come through its website (often an important consumer touch point), it's critical to include on the innovation team a representative from the department charged with designing the website. Similarly, if phone support is a key feature of a company's new service, a representative of the customer service department should be on the innovation team.

In some cases, companies initially don't know which functions and departments will be important to include. The team member descriptions that follow represent the core participants we think are important to any innovation, working backward from the customer's point of view to company operations.

Brand Management

Typically responsible for some of the closest interactions with consumers, brand management should be an integral part of the innovation team, even at the earliest stages of developing a meaningful customer experience. The brand team can ensure that customers perceive a company's meaning as it is intended. This is no small contribution, and in many cases makes the difference between a product being a category leader and a category loser—even when it is functionally similar to others in the marketplace. If no one charged with building the brand is included until the product or service is almost fully developed (this is a common practice among technology firms), the positioning, advertising, product placement, pricing, promotional activity, and other aspects of brand communication will likely seem artificial and inauthentic. If the company is a start-up and doesn't yet have brand management, a brand consultant should play this role.

Sales Management

This function is almost always overlooked in the innovation process, but that's a serious mistake if a company is truly committed to connecting to its customers through meaningful experiences. In thousands of companies, salespeople represent a firm's human face to the world, whether behind a counter at McDonald's or on the phone selling mutual funds. In organizations that serve primarily large business accounts like Cisco and Alcoa, direct sales firms such as Avon or Discovery Toys, and retailing companies like Gap or Pizza Hut, sales personnel are the closest contact to the consumer. As such, they are often the first to see opportunities for or problems with new or improved experiences and threats to existing ones. For companies that sell through retail channels, sales management's intimacy with retailers can help an innovation team better understand how to enhance the customer's experience at point of purchase by anticipating the conditions of that environment.

Unfortunately, because they are rewarded or given incentives based on what they can sell today, salespeople tend to focus on the short term. This often drives them to be tactical and conservative, reluctant to endorse change unless something is clearly wrong. Since much of the front-end labor of designing meaningful customer experiences demands an openness to discovering new opportunities, exploring new ideas, and asking new questions, the process can be challenging for the person representing the sales function. Nevertheless, getting his or her support and buy-in is important. Sales management needs to understand and embrace any new experience opportunities a firm pursues. If not, sales personnel can greatly detract from a customer's experience, either directly by not supporting the delivery of the experience as the company intends, or inadvertently because they don't know how.

Marketing Management and Research

Some companies combine the brand and marketing functions. On an innovation team, however, it may make more sense to have them represented separately. A marketing manager (or in some companies, a market planner) can identify where new opportunities lie. He or she can recognize what types of experiences customers will value and how best to deliver them. This contributor brings needed viewpoints about marketplace trends, current customer base, distribution channels, and corporate capabilities.

Marketing managers ensure there is a real, paying customer waiting on the other end of the process. This team member helps prevent development of products and services that are "cool" and interesting to their developers but fill no real need in the marketplace.

An important part of most marketing departments is the research or customer-insight team. This group is generally charged with gathering, analyzing and centralizing all the company's intelligence around its customers and the broader market of potential customers. In companies where the team gathering customer insights is lead by a strong, strategic thinker who values exploratory research, this person should certainly be included on the innovation team. In companies where the team gathering insights plays more of an administrative role, tracking or auditing past purchasing behavior, their leader will probably not be able to contribute until later in the innovation process when evaluation and validation measures are needed.

Design

The title "designer" means different things in different organizations, and it can sometimes encompass far-reaching responsibilities. Here we're referring to those people charged with conceiving the overall product idea and the principal characteristics of the intended customer experience. In some companies, this role is in marketing; in other companies, it's in R&D, engineering, or the design department. In some cases, it's the job of the CEO or the entrepreneurial inventor.

The people charged with conceiving the innovation are rarely left off innovation teams. In fact, designers are frequently the only people on them, and that can doom an innovation process before it starts. But as members of a more cross-functional team, concept designers often struggle to find their role. They are generally accustomed to exercising more direct control over the innovation process, so it's awkward for them to share that responsibility with others. Conceding to requests of marketing, brand, engineering, or others may cause designers to worry about threats to the integrity and viability of their ideas. However, designers who stay closely connected to customers and who are inspired and guided by them can continue to drive their company's innovation process despite sharing this responsibility. In fact, by aligning with other departments, they can gain both power and influence to ensure that the experience they envision for customers has the best chance of becoming real.

Development

By development, we mean any process that actually builds the concept or solution envisioned by design. In a technology company, this might be software engineering or industrial design. In a food company, the developers might be chemists or food technologists, while in a financial services company, the developers might be economists or mathematicians. Regardless of their skill set, developers typically work toward the same goal as designers and marketers, but they work on the back end of the experience—that is, the system, product composition, or whatever delivers the functional part of the consumer's perception of the experience. While developers' work may seem hidden or less prominent, their contribution dramatically impacts the user experience. If the production specs aren't grounded in customer understanding, the product or service can end up working against the desired experience and its underlying meaning. For example, Microsoft's infamous introduction of the "Bob" operating system and Coke's equally awkward misstep with New Coke underscore the inability of marketing and brand efforts to carry the full burden of meaning. If the product or service doesn't really deliver on the promised experience, other attributes can't make up for it. On the other hand, LeapFrog, a company that develops technology intended for use by young children, makes products that are so well designed and engineered that they typically deliver more than their marketing promises and exceed customers' expectations.

Design and development functions need to work hand in hand throughout the innovation process. Neither side can claim more importance and neither should be underrepresented within the process. Engineers working on back-end implementations can suggest some of the most important customer-centric interactions. Likewise, it's not uncommon for astute front-end developers to suggest an improvement to the back-end system.

Information Technology (IT)

A company's information technology department is not usually connected to the innovation process, but it has an important role to

play in the development of meaningful customer experiences. Ultimately, the more a company's information system mirrors and supports its innovation process, rather than only supporting production
or finances, the faster and more efficiently a company's experience
innovation process will run. By making real-time information about
customer needs and desires available for the team to access, IT can
smooth the decision-making process. Likewise, IT systems can facil-
itate more effective collaboration by enabling communication
across time and distance, by providing searchable archives of past
work, and by facilitating creation of digital prototypes and rapidly
rendered concepts.

Human Resources

It's unusual for a company to include human resources in its innovation process, but it's worth considering. In its responsibility for
recruiting and nurturing everyone within the organization, HR representatives often understand better than others how important the
company's delivery of meaning is. HR managers may not play a
direct role in the innovation process, but they are indispensable in
the delivery and maintenance of customer experiences because these
experiences come from a company's employees, as well as its products and services. This is more obvious with service companies, such
as UPS, United Airlines, and Citibank, where part of the product is
the employees' interaction with customers, but it's just as true for
employees at product-oriented companies. Every employee ultimately represents his or her company and contributes to customers'
perceptions. As such, HR personnel should be watchful that corporate messages are effectively communicated and clearly understood.
They should constantly be asking for clarification of goals as they
relate to human resources needs—especially hiring. No matter how
talented an employee may be, if he doesn't fit the culture or embrace
the corporate processes, he will impede corporate goals for delivering meaningful experiences to the customer.

Operations

Chief operating officers and others in operations are usually thought of as the people responsible for maintaining the status quo and keeping it running smoothly. However, they are often the best informed about time, energy, and expenditures, and the relationships of these to goals, strategies, and results. While people in operations don't often have first-hand knowledge of customer needs and desires, they are in a unique position to highlight what the company says it wants to do, what it really does, and how these actions impact its overall performance.

On a cross-disciplinary innovation team, an operations manager can ensure that the drive to create meaningful experiences is translated throughout the organization and becomes an ongoing way of doing business.

CEOs

The chief executive officer may not be able to take part in every company conversation about customers, meaning, or experiences, but his or her support for the overall goal needs to be highly evident. The CEO needs to understand the goal, define what success looks like, and hold the team accountable for achieving it.

Ideally, to evoke meaning for customers, the CEO needs to embody that same meaning through his personality, his actions, and in his public speaking—as Herb Kelleher did for Southwest Air and as Steve Jobs does for Apple. Often this is the easiest and fastest way for employees to understand what a meaningful experience entails and how to deliver it to the company's customers.

Making Decisions

There's one role we didn't include in our list of innovation team members: the lead decision maker.

Assembling the right team is an important step, but the team can't function without leadership and decision-making. In fact, some of the worst innovation processes we've seen are those using "virtual" cross-functional teams where no designated leader is in charge. In these cases the innovation process becomes chaotic. Some departments struggle to outdo the rest, others passively resist, and a few valiantly try to make the process

> Regardless of who assumes this task, the leader needs to be guided by a singular focus on the customer.

work. Even though all the functions of innovation are included, they have no means to work together effectively and no one understands why the process—which they have so consciously instigated—isn't working. Worse yet, this discourages the company from doing it again and it reverts back to old behaviors.

A leader can come from almost any of the collaborating functions. In addition to possessing the essential leadership qualities of ambition, confidence, clarity of vision, and communication skills, he or she will need to be an excellent collaboration facilitator and should understand the roles and responsibilities of all the different departments included in the process.

Leaving aside personality traits, certain members of an organization make the best leaders for an initiative in innovation. Top among them is the CEO, particularly if the company is relatively small. The innovation process we're discussing will be central to the future of the business and the CEO is the only person with the near-guaranteed ability to get regular, consistent attention placed on the process. A divisional president might play the same role in a larger company.

The head of marketing may also make a good leader, particularly if she is seen as an innovator and someone focused on the customer. The head of design could also be a good choice, provided that he can transcend the limited definition of "design" as simply meaning appearance. Similarly, the head of development can be an effective leader if he isn't so enamored of his technology or science that customers' needs and desires are ignored. We'd also like to put in a good word for the chief financial officer. This might seem like a surprising option, but CFOs are often the most effective people at cutting through detail and getting to core issues.

Regardless of who assumes this task, the leader needs to be guided by a singular focus on the customer. This perspective may derive from research, experience, or inspiration, but a customer orientation must be the determining factor in all decisions related to the delivery of meaningful experiences.

Five

Designing Meaningful Experiences

The design of meaningful experiences can be integrated into almost any innovation process, but to do so requires a new way of thinking about development and its effect. Rather than thinking of design as a function limited to visual expression or engineering, we need to recognize design conceptually as both the intent and the process of integrating functional, economic, emotional, or social benefits within a meaningful context. It is through design that a company can align with changing consumer values and convey a coherent and correctly perceived experience through the full range of marketing, interaction, and communication media.

"Design" is a confusing word. To some, it conjures up images of clothing. To others, it is preceded by the word "interior" and guides the selection of couches and window coverings. To still others, it might be a fancy or beautiful product, car, or logo—the result of a singular genius with a unique vision. As these descriptions suggest, design is most often associated with appearance, seldom with performance.

As we've done with the concepts of "meaning" and "experience," we want to clarify our definition of "design." We have said that design covers a range of disciplines and produces a myriad of results. But in all its manifestations, design identifies and builds value based on a deep understanding of customer needs. This definition of design applies not only to decisions of appearance (such as color, typeface, material, and form), though of course these are critical. It also relates to levels of performance (such as process, workflow, interaction, and experience). Furthermore, it applies at the level of business itself, including corporate strategy, structure, process, and goals. So when we speak of design, we are talking about a mechanism for consciously creating value based on truly understanding customers as people and, ideally, caring about, having empathy for, and being compassionate toward them. Design techniques offer businesses ways to identify customer needs and desires specifically so they can address them through their products, services, and events, yielding experiences that are valuable to both customers and companies.

Design Intent

This broader definition of design should not be confused with invention, which does not require the production of value to customers or solutions that are driven by customer needs and desires. In fact, inventions are often demonstrations of capability—scientists and engineers often invent something new because they can, not necessarily to fill a need in the market place. Invention is possible in almost any field, including art, science, entertainment, and education; but only design, as we define it, is expressly committed to the creation of customer value and meaning.

As such, design, when practiced well, employs a set of research techniques and processes for understanding people and problems, generating solutions, and testing concepts against customer value—all before the implementation and delivery of an actual product. The design process offers businesses ways of discussing and delivering value in the widest possible contexts—approaches to improve the conversations within an organization, and as a result, the decisions organizations make. Managers can rely on the design process to give them new, powerful, and important insights—not only into their markets and customers, but also into their own organizations and their industry. Through the collaborative, deliberative process that it demands and reinforces, design can become a business leader's ally in transforming an organization, its offerings, and its markets, as well as differentiating its products, services, and customer experiences. As such, any firm not employing and integrating design techniques into its regimen is crippling its ability to succeed.

To successfully develop meaningful experiences, this appreciation of design's role and power—which we've articulated into seven principles—needs to take root in the company and guide the innovation process.

1. Design creates corporate value. One of the most powerful properties of the design process is the way it helps a team articulate, and hence, realize intent—to make meaning real for customers and for the company. Organizations determine their future by first defining a vision of what is possible and desirable, then using design as the muscle to move that vision beyond a diagram or a set of bullet points to a reality.

By focusing the organization on the power of design, we drive better products, services, and experiences, but we also impact the corporate culture. Employees become more aware of the company's meaning and better able to support it, regardless of their job title. It's this awareness that prompts delivery people to praise their company's products to complete strangers or telephone support personnel to address each caller with care. Similarly, an awareness of their company's meaning can help employees better understand its company's actions, defend its occasional missteps, and generally feel more engaged and part of a team. On a recent trip, Cheskin's CEO arrived at the Alaska Airlines departure gate late for his flight because his printed itinerary showed an incorrect time. The desk agent on duty could have tried to blame the travel agent, but instead she sympathized with his problem, immediately gave him a voucher for food, helped him find another flight, and explained that he could relax in Alaska Airline's Board Room for a small daily fee. She didn't need to get authorization or check her rule book. She knew instinctively how the company wanted her to react.

2. Design is pervasive. One of the worst things a company can do is to keep the design function relegated to an individual, a small group, or even worse, a list of rules. Think of the design process as a beneficial virus that is most useful when it spreads throughout your organization. By this reasoning, anyone who builds value based on customer understandings is, in effect, a designer. Think of design as the best conversation you and your organization can have, one that involves all aspects of your business, with an emphasis on your customers' needs.

Instead of appointing a design czar or narrowly defined design department, a better approach is for all departments to be design oriented, with an experienced person or council of experienced people who are made responsible for developing and communicating best practices and experience guidelines. This approach allows design to function properly as a shared language of collaboration, rather than something applied by a special person or group. For example, at Cheskin, we have three experience guidelines that govern everyone's work: Learn, Collaborate, Inspire. These guidelines are elaborated in posters that hang on the wall and explained in depth on our internal website. Small committees create work sessions and exercises that help employees understand how to bring each guideline into their daily activities. Everyone's annual review includes a section that evaluates their support of these guidelines. Throughout the company, this shared language helps shape goals and direct decisions.

3. Design is collaborative. The image of a designer working alone or commanding a team of subordinates is a myth. In reality, design is the synthesis of multiple opinions and perspectives, carefully balanced constraints, and considerable revision. Since effective solutions can come from different directions, it's the interplay between people that makes the difference between bad, good, and great design. Instilling and supporting diversity on the design team is critical, as is fostering a collaborative environment that is open to the expression of divergent viewpoints.

Keep in mind that when we speak of diversity, we mean more than skin color. A mixture of ages and genders is as important as a mixture of cultural perspectives. Particularly in business environments, it is often the woman's perspective or that of a 25- year-old that is missing from design collaborations. Ironically and unfortunately, these perspectives typically reflect large and important consumer constituencies.

4. Design includes execution. Companies often treat ideas as if they were the end-point instead of the beginning of a process. But ideas in and of themselves aren't valuable and make no contribution to a company until they are elaborated enough to be patented or until they take shape in the marketplace. It is the execution of an idea that, ultimately, changes businesses or the world. Reward the development, deployment, and delivery of ideas that provide actual value to your customers.

Microsoft took a step in this direction recently, basing senior executive bonuses not just on improved sales numbers, but also on an improvement in customer satisfaction levels. Since customers are rarely satisfied by an idea alone, this clearly communicated a corporate commitment to successful execution.

5. Design is a transparent, knowable process. To non-designers, the design process may seem mysterious and inaccessible. Some designers might welcome this "unknowability," feeling that it protects them from scrutiny and conveys a sense of status, but ultimately it hurts designers because it alienates them from others and makes people distrust their contributions.

Far from being mysterious or unknowable, true design can be quantified and qualified. Furthermore, designers can be held accountable for meeting clear specifications and helping the team achieve its stated goals. Everyone involved in the innovation process—especially designers—should be able to discuss why they made certain choices. More often than not, a choice should hinge on whether it provides customer value. Those who can't explain their choices, or worse, refuse to and hide behind "inspiration," with no customer validation, shouldn't be trusted to make decisions.

6. Design is iterative. The perfect solution is impossible, but design techniques that allow sufficient time for iteration greatly reduce errors and heighten success. By allowing time for review and refinement of ideas, concepts, frameworks, prototypes, and communications, a firm increases the likelihood that the final outcome will be a success.

At the same time, remember that the greatest improvements in design come in the first few iterations. After that, the significance of each version usually declines to the point where there is no significant value gained. Design teams need to locate that mid-point where the benefits of iteration are not exceeded its costs.

7. Design includes both short-tern and long-term goals. Properly implemented, design can support both a company's short-term needs and its long-term goals. In its ability to solve problems and attract attention, design's contributions can show up in short-term metrics, such as quarterly financials, product launch revenue, or last month's brand awareness. But just as important, design can lay a foundation of increasing growth and profitability by providing a blueprint for future generations of products, services, and connections.

By adopting these principles and using them throughout the innovation process, the design of meaningful experiences can become a company-wide effort. With these principles in place, the

The Innovation Process

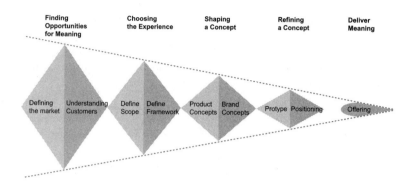

FIGURE 5.1: The process for designing meaningful experiences proceeds through five phases, starting with a broad exploration of opportunity and progressing to the final detailed expression through products, services, brand and all other consumer touch points.

process outlined in the following section can become a respected and acceptable approach to pursuing new opportunity and building stronger, more resilient consumer relationships.

The Process

The design principles we've explained reflect an emerging philosophy that design is a process that can reliably build value for customers, using a repeatable process with a testable outcome. We believe the innovation team will succeed to the extent the members live by these principles and the team follows a systematic approach similar to the one we'll outline next. The innovation team we described in the previous chapter will succeed to the extent that it operates by these principles.

The design of meaningful experiences begins by identifying the opportunity for new or improved connections to meaning and concludes with the expression and ongoing support of that meaning through a multitude of consumer touch points. The earliest stages are concentrated on developing strategies, ideas, frameworks, themes, guidelines, and prototypes, while the latter stages elaborate on refinements, details, options, connections, and communications. Both development and marketing are involved throughout, with design being the shared language for collaboration.

We'll explore each of these stages in more depth in upcoming chapters, but for those of you who prefer CliffsNotes, here is an overview of the process:

1. Identify the opportunity. With over 6 billion people presently sharing the planet, there's no shortage of demand for meaningful experiences. The challenge is finding the demand you can authentically and profitably fill.

This stage identifies how, where, and when people want or need to connect to new or deeper experiences. Where are the openings or gaps that your company could fill—not with products, but with experiences? How large is the opportunity and how rapidly is it growing? What's motivating this demand and how pervasive is it? This is the stage for carefully examining your competitors' offerings, seeing where they succeed and where they fail. This is also the stage for understanding market dynamics, in particular the distribution system, the supply chain, and the means of communicating with likely customers.

You'd be surprised how many companies skip this critical phase. Usually it's because managers think they already know the marketplace well enough to speculate, or because they've already decided there's a market for the offering they have. Both of these assumptions are risky unless backed up by solid evidence. Market knowledge should be current, comprehensive, and fully identified before moving to the next stage. It should be informed by meaning and not merely attitude, usage, lifestyle or price preference. If not, a company risks wasting its development time and money to build experiences that aren't valued sufficiently to repay the investment.

Typically, by spending three months or less, you can identify whether a reasonable market opportunity exists, produce a rough outline of its nature, truly understand your potential customer's needs and desires and give the team confidence to move forward.

2. Frame the business idea. Once the opportunity is identified, a company needs to envision and scope out how it plans to act on that opportunity. This is the stage for creating a plan, putting together a budget, assembling a team, setting deadlines, and considering all aspects of execution. This is the "constraint" stage, when companies put boundaries around an opportunity or an idea in order to make it possible. Skipping this stage is not just risky, it's disastrous. Without a framework to scope development, team members are clueless about the end goal. There's no blueprint to follow and no real means for making decisions.

3. Shape the experience concept. This is the stage at which the innovation team conceptualizes the experience a company hopes to evoke. It often begins as a simple observation of people's desire. Method, the innovative household products company we talked about earlier, developed its experience concept from an insight about people loving to care for their home. At this stage the idea is transformed to its full expression.

Companies differ in how they conceptualize. Some brainstorm, others are more analytical. Some depend heavily on consumer input, while others avoid it at this stage. We've seen each approach work successfully, provided the innovation team is well organized, highly collaborative, and capable of producing clear, well thought-out comps or prototypes that accurately depict the full range of the consumer's experience.

At this stage it's important to keep in mind that meaningful experiences are delivered through the full range of consumer touch points, that they should be consistent and integrated, and that you want to leave some level of customization for the consumer. Both developers and marketers need to equally participate in this stage.

They need to agree on what the experience is and the mechanisms by which it's evoked.

4. Refine the experience. While some firms may prefer to fast-forward to the product launch rather than take time to refine the experience, this stage is absolutely critical to consumers' final perceptions of the experience. This is the detail stage, where the nuances and fine points of meaning are worked out. Attention to this stage raises the likelihood that potential customers will correctly understand and appreciate the experience being offered, rather than being confused or dismissive.

Typically this is the stage when firms turn to their markets for feedback (although we recommend including consumer feedback from the very beginning of this process). Large firms will test their products and services, as well as imagery, pricing, packaging, messaging, interface design, and all the other interactions with potential customers. Smaller firms may just test the product or service. In either case, if done appropriately, this type of research will indicate how the market at large will respond. It's a smart company that uses this feedback as a way to adjust and refine the experience, not just as a disaster check.

5. Expressing the experience. This final stage of the design process delivers and maintains the full impact of the experience, both in the market place and within the company. This is the stage of active, outbound marketing that communicates and attracts the right customers, that convinces them to try something new, better, different or similar. This is also the stage that continues the connection over time, building a stronger relationship through repeated experiences. While it's tempting to launch a new offering and judge its success by the initial response, most meaningful experiences take some time to develop. The first Starbucks, the first shoes from Nike, the first Disneyland, and the first Bank of America—all were starting points on evolutionary processes that continue to this day.

This stage nurtures and evolves the experience in response to customers, competitors, new technology, trends and anything else that influences it. You should consider omitting this stage only if the company has a death wish.

We've explained these steps as simply as possible, but we've left out considerable detail that is important to consider in adopting this practice. In the coming chapters, we'll take each stage and explain how we approach them, how they build and connect with each other, and what types of outcome each produces.

Six

Identifying the Opportunity for Meaning

The design of authentically meaningful experiences emerges from a deep understanding of the potential customer. It also requires a keen appreciation of market and industry dynamics, as well as influential technology and design trends. From the cultural perspective, we identify how, where, when, and why people want to connect to new or deeper experiences. From the business perspective, we learn what it will take to be financially and commercially successful. The understanding we gain from these two perspectives defines how a new experience is delivered and provides a standard by which to evaluate the potential business impact of that offering.

Both perspectives—business and cultural—are equally important and interdependent. In our experience, it doesn't matter whether a company starts with one or the other, as long as both are taken into account. We'll begin with the market assessment from the business perspective.

Defining the Market

Assessing market opportunity is a significant but fairly common business activity, so we won't spend much time describing it. It's a straightforward process that defines the industry, determines its size and growth rate, and identifies key trends and enabling technologies. A market assessment also studies the distribution system, supply chain, and communication channels. A good assessment carefully examines competitors' offerings as well, objectively noting where they succeed and where they fall short.

A market assessment is an important component in making meaning because it helps clarify the level of investment and commitment a company will need to make to successfully deliver experiences within a particular industry. The assessment provides valuable information for setting realistic goals, defining boundaries, determining partnerships or alliances, and integrating appropriate trends and technology.

A truly useful market assessment is built using current, comprehensive data. Fortunately, these details are in abundant supply thanks to the Internet, industry analysts, a company's archives, and search engines. Analyst estimates of market size, growth rate, and major trends are readily available for most industries. Some companies have a single, trusted source of market information, but our preference is to build an overview of an industry by digesting and comparing several estimates. At a minimum, the data should outline the following:

- What is the size of the current market, and how large is it expected to grow over the next three to five years?
- What are the main categories within the industry, including their size and growth rates?
- Who are the key players, and what are their business strategies? Which companies are positioned to enter the industry, even though they are not currently competitors?
- What major trends are shaping the future direction of the market (social, cultural, regulatory, and so on)?
- What technologies or new capabilities are being adopted, and by whom?

- What is the overall profile of the target audience, and what distinct types of customer is each major competitor targeting?
- What are the core customer needs that this industry addresses?
- Which channels serve the industry and what is purchase process?

A market assessment that answers these questions creates a framework for looking at the business dynamics and clarifies the starting point for innovation and design. For example, imagine we lead the innovation team for a company we'll call Footwork, Inc. that makes athletic shoes. An overview like this would tell us that the current U.S. shoe market has roughly $40 billion in sales and is characterized by slow growth, brand fragmentation, and domination by large national and multinational marketers. Such an assessment would let us know that casual shoes make up half the market, athletic shoes another third, with the rest divided between dress shoes and rugged shoes (like hiking boots). We'd know that children's shoes comprise 18 percent of the market; that nine out every ten shoes is imported; that shoe stores account for 30 percent of sales; and that consumer advertising for shoes exceeds $500 million a year. We'd understand the latest technical inventions and the popular style trends.

In other words, we'd have a good understanding of the nuts and bolts of the footwear industry. But we wouldn't yet know anything about our potential customer's experience of wearing shoes, nor what is (or could be) meaningful about that experience. For that kind of information we need to assess the opportunity from a consumer's point of view, emphasizing a cultural and personal perspective.

Understanding the Customer

Learning what is meaningful to your potential customers isn't easy. Unlike the business analysis, data on consumer experiences and valued meanings is usually more difficult to find. We can't Google "experience of accomplishment," or "what meanings people value," and hope to get much help. Even companies that have a great deal of customer information rarely get to this level of discernment. But by spending a modest amount of time, effort, and investment, this type of assessment can provide fundamental and powerful understandings of not only who a company's customers are, but also how meaning shapes their world.

Learning what is meaningful to customers can rely on a variety of research tools, but the process must always be wide-ranging and exploratory. Research can be conducted by a company's internal research department, or by an external partner with specific expertise. Regardless of who is responsible for the research and how it's performed, the researchers doing this work should have a robust, vivid understanding of what meaningful experiences are, and they should structure their fieldwork around three questions:

- What types of meaningful experiences do customers want?
- What experiences are currently offered in the marketplace?
- How can a desired meaning be delivered?

Getting to Meaning

Exploring what the role meaning has in their lives and the types of experiences people want can be an overwhelming task unless the process is organized in a manageable way and tied to a reasonable business goal. For example, one typical approach is to begin by profiling potential customers and categorizing them into groups or segments that share similar traits. Conventional segmentation typically divides people into demographic or psychographic groupings, and then prioritizes those groups according to which are most likely to buy a company's products or services. Meaning-based segmentation, on the other hand, groups people by their meaning preferences and then chooses which groups to serve.

When the goal is to segment and profile consumers by the meanings they value, personal interviewing is mandatory. Observation alone can often be misinterpreted, and structured surveys by phone or online can't provide enough depth and clarity. The most popular approaches to conducting personal interviews are ethnographic methods adapted from anthropology. Ethnography, as we practice it, means the holistic study of a person's experience, meaning-making, and behavior in the context of daily life. In simplest terms, an ethnographer spends extended periods of time observing and interviewing people while they go about the business of living their lives. They enter a person's home, workplace, or other representative environment and observe whatever activities are relevant with particular care to context and processes. While traditional interviewers ask about how the person feels, what they are thinking, how they make choices, and what products or services they would prefer, ethnographic researchers also look beyond the person to also observe the environment—its sounds, smells, and its appearance. One reason this type of research works well at uncovering people's preference for meaning is that it gets at what people really feel and do "in the moment," rather than what they say at a later time. Ethnography also gives researchers access to subtle details and nuances that are important to understand, but which often remain unseen or taken for granted.

Let's return to Footwork, our hypothetical shoe company to see how this works. We would start our meaning-based segmentation process by conducting ethnographic interviews with a range of potential customers. Our ethnographers would visit a consumer's home and see his shoes. The interview would begin broadly, talking about lifestyle, activities, and possibly notions of play and work. It would narrow to clothing needs, style, footwear, athletic pursuits, perhaps ideals of beauty or creativity in fashion. The ethnographer would ask to see the person's shoes and while looking at them would ask for details about how, when and why each was purchased or is worn. This exploration and discussion usually lasts two to three hours.

Despite ethnography's effectiveness, observation and open-ended interviews aren't always sufficient to uncover meaning. Sometimes it takes creative techniques, such as improvisation, laddering or indirect questioning. Laddering is an interview approach used to reveal the underlying reasons people prefer a product, brand, or feature. This kind of interview begins with the rational preferences people easily identify like functional and economic benefits, then "ladders up" to broader values that are tapped by that preference.

In using this approach, the ethnographer working on the shoe company account might observe a person choosing a particular model of athletic shoe in a store and ask, "What features do you like about that shoe?" The consumer might point to the functional design of the sole and its cushioning details. The ethnographer would then ask, "Why is the design of the sole important to you?" At this point, the person being interviewed might hesitate for a moment, and then explain that he cares about how his foot feels when it hits the ground. Again the ethnographer asks (sometimes sounding a bit like a 5 year-old), "Why is how your foot feels when it hits the ground important to you?" The person responds that if his foot feels good when it hits the ground, he feels more powerful and has the energy to go further. This explanation of emotional benefits prompts the ethnographer to ask another follow-up question, "Why is feeling powerful and going further important to you?" The shoe shopper explains that achieving goals is a meaningful part of his life. If there is a meaningful connection to be found, this kind of interview, though simple and methodical, can often find it.

Unfortunately, in many instances, direct questioning doesn't work. Some aspects of meaning are better found through indirectly questioning. Indirect questioning avoids specific questions about meaning and instead explores related behaviors, attitudes, beliefs and other evidence that can reveal the role meaning plays in a person's life. For example, our Footwork ethnographer might ask a consumer to use photographs to answer questions like "My feet are happiest when they look like this," or "This helps me look my best." Photos can uncover insights and deeper meaning that people might otherwise forget or be unable to convey in words. They also allow ethnographers to see places and experiences normally hidden from view. For example, we used this technique to gain a deeper perspective on what people do when they are in the shower. For obvious reasons, no one wanted an ethnographer observing them in the shower, but many agreed to share more discreet photos and other visuals that represented how they felt about the experience. Our ethnographers used those images to guide a discussion that uncovered four different segments of "shower takers," each of whom found different meaning in that daily ritual.

Another form of indirect questioning that can effectively get at deeper meaning are projective techniques. For example, in work we did for the *St. Louis Post-Dispatch,* we asked people to imagine that a new newspaper suddenly appeared that had an uncanny ability to publish stories that always interested them. In short, it was each person's ideal newspaper. We then asked which of their photos the paper would publish and what the story would say. In the telling of the answers we learned the deeper meaning of the photo (and for this client, what the most meaningful news experience was about).

Choosing and Confirming

Many different approaches and techniques can help find the opportunity for meaning and even more will be developed in the coming years. but we're going to assume you get the point and move to the equally important step of using these insights to better understand the market opportunity.

Our shoe company has completed the initial exploration and learned that potential customers divide into five distinct groups of adult shoe buyers, based on the type of meaningful experience each seeks. As members of the innovation team, we would decide which groups represent the best opportunities for Footwork based on the size of the group, its growth rate, its potential profitability, the likelihood of competition or the company's desire or ability to offer that particular meaningful experience. In some cases, a company might try to serve two or three groups with a combined experience. Nike does that by offering athletic footwear that can be customized, serving both a desire for accomplishment and creation. Rarely would a company decide to design one experience to suit more than three groups because the experience would then become too complex or diluted.

Although ethnography and other forms of qualitative interviewing are most effective at identifying the demand for meaning and the nature of desirable experiences, neither of these approaches is useful for estimating the size or value of the opportunity. Consequently, ethnographic work is often followed by quantitative research that surveys large numbers of people and uses statistical rigor to provide more precise measurements and predictions.

As with ethnography, there are numerous quantitative techniques we find to be effective. Whether they are done online, by phone, or in person, the important thing is that they suit the needs of the company and that they be done well. Quantitative techniques are only reliable if the correct population of people is interviewed, the right questions are asked, and they are asked in the appropriate way. These may seem like basic criteria, but we've seen many development processes undermined by faulty quantitative research that gave false assurances of success, or conversely, inaccurately warned of failure.

What are the right questions to confirm the demand for an experience? Normally, if the ethnographic research is done first, it suggests which areas are most important to validate. However, conveying a desirable experience through words is an art. Asking someone, "Do you choose an athletic shoe to give you a sense of accomplishment—yes or no?" is unlikely to elicit accurate, or even usable data. For that reason, we advocate using indirect questioning and when possible, using visuals to convey the nature of an experience. Our footwear company might show a series of images suggesting the concepts of accomplishment, creation, unity, freedom, and validation. Under each visual we'd list statements like "reflects an important quality to consider" or "most like me." We'd ask people to review each image and then rate the accuracy of each statement. Testing the questionnaire on a small sampling of people can ensure that each visual is understood as intended.

Dozens of techniques like the ones we've described can work to uncover meaning in people's lives, and to explore the full range of experiences people have and want. Regardless of the research approach a company adopts, the outcome should explain how consumers differ in the type of experiences they desire, and bring the identity of those potential customers into sharp focus. At the end of this phase of innovation, researchers should be able to state their beliefs about possible market appeal on a segment-by-segment basis. They should also be encouraged to propose initial product direction and ideas based on their understanding of what consumers want. While it's too early for ethnographers and researchers to tell an innovation team exactly what to do at this point, they can collaborate with the innovation team to make sense of what the market is saying.

Combining these two assessments—the market perspective and the consumer perspective—gives companies and their innovation teams a complete landscape of the opportunity available to them. The next step takes this broad, more exploratory view and frames the specific opportunity the company wants to address.

Seven

Framing the Experience

I dentifying the market opportunity for meaningful experiences illustrates the options open to a company. The next step is to clearly define what a company will create to pursue that opportunity. In this stage, we do that by answering questions that only the company itself can decide: Which opportunity—and specifically, which meaning—represents the best fit to the company's goals and abilities? How should the company integrate functional, economic, emotional or identity attributes into the experience? What resources can the company devote to this pursuit, and over what period of time? How will success be measured? These answers start to form a framework for the innovation process, one that is increasingly refined and made richer as the process continues.

This stage requires the innovation team to set boundaries that can be difficult for some members to accept because it means some opportunities must be abandoned or scaled down. The process of eliminating some and focusing on just one or two is a beneficial one, however, because through it, an opportunity becomes an attainable goal. This stage also requires initial financial and business scope planning. When it comes to the financial evaluation of opportunities and the basics of product planning, hundreds of books and thousands of consultants can provide guidance on estimating revenue and return, developing a business model, establishing timelines, and creating alliances for outsourcing, licensing or partnering. We won't dwell on these details other than to confirm they are important early decisions. What we want to do in this chapter instead is to concentrate on additional considerations we believe are necessary when planning the design of meaningful experiences.

In the previous chapter our shoe company, Footwork, discovered consumer segments with five distinct preferences for meaningful experiences that the company could potentially use as a focus for its innovation. We also determined that the market dynamics support further innovation in this category. Now we need to decide which opportunities the company will pursue and to what extent. Let's assume the company quickly decided to ignore two of the consumer segments: one is too small, and the other does not have a good fit with the company's direction. The three remaining segments include consumers who seek the experience of accomplishment, those who seek the experience of beauty, and those who seek the experience of freedom—all promise strong potential, but can the company address all three segments and if so, how should the desired experiences be combined into a cohesive and appealing offer? Choosing the consumer target and defining the scope of the experience will begin to create the framework for the process which ensues.

Choosing the Experience

Sometimes just the process of thinking about the customer in a new, experiential way makes it relatively easy for innovation team members to choose and define the experiences they want to offer. At this point, a company may realize it already offers its customers a meaningful experience but is not delivering it as completely and cohesively as it could. Perhaps its brand conveys meaning, but its product doesn't really live up to that promise. Or perhaps its service and brand evoke a sense of community for customers, but contact with customer support feels like this is only marketing hype and not something the company truly believes. In this situation, making the choice of which experience to offer may be a relatively simple one: the innovation team confirms the desire to continue offering the same experience, but with better execution and attention to detail throughout the company.

In other cases, the decision is more complex. It's not unusual for a company's research to show that its consumers want experiences from a company that are in conflict with one another. In a recent project for a major software company, we found its customers expressing a desire for both a sense of security and a sense of freedom. The innovation team needed to decide which of these conflicting experiences was most important to deliver because it couldn't realistically deliver both: if it truly delivered an experience of freedom, it would likely compromise the experience of security, and vice versa.

Another fairly common and frustrating hurdle many companies face is not being able to deliver a desired experience because that solution simply doesn't exist yet. Most people would love to have a greater experience of freedom using their cell phones—being assured the device will work anywhere, whether that means a foreign country, or a fast-moving elevator. The cell phone concept implicitly promises this, but as of right now competing feature sets and dueling industry standards make the delivery of that experience incomplete, frustrating probably every cell user.

When choosing which consumers to pursue and what type of experience to deliver, at a minimum a company should confirm the following:

- There is an identifiable consumer segment that desires a meaningful experience. The company should be able to describe these consumers in a very clear and detailed manner. In fact, the consumer profile should be rich and ani-

mated enough for members of the innovation team to recognize them as real people—rather than percentages or
data points.

- The segment desiring the experience is large enough to
  meet the company's financial criteria for success. Early
  adopters are attractive but unless their interests and actions
  are likely to be followed by a much larger audience, they
  don't represent a viable segment for long-term growth and
  positive financial return.

- The experience the segment desires is not in conflict with
  anything else the company does. For example, as Kraft
  Foods began moving toward its current vision of "helping
  people around the world eat and live better" it was in the
  awkward position of being owned by the world's largest
  tobacco company, Phillip Morris (now Altria Group) under
  indictment for endangering people's lives. This conflict of
  values was somewhat mitigated when Altria Group spun off
  Kraft Foods as an independent company (although Altria
  still owns most of Kraft, the conflict is now less apparent to
  Kraft's customers).

- The experience does not over-promise, but rather is an
  accurate reflection of the company's capabilities. Meaningful experiences are not a new flavor of marketing hype.
  If a company can't really commit to delivering the experience in a full, robust and cohesive way, it will likely fall
  flat. This doesn't mean companies have to be perfect and
  never take risks. It just means they should be authentic in
  their goals and intentions. For example, many companies
  believe they can attract Hispanic consumers by just translating their ads from English to Spanish without understanding the cultural differences that influence this
  market. While this occasionally works, it often doesn't

because the intended audience can tell the communication and by association, the product or service, is inauthentic.

If an innovation team can't find an experience that meets these criteria or can't overcome the hurdles we've discussed, then regardless of the team's enthusiasm for the idea of producing a meaningful customer experience, it is not time yet to go forward.

Defining Scope

Let's say Footwork decides it can effectively serve both the consumer segment that values accomplishment and the segment that values beauty. The two meanings are compatible, and the company believes it has the credibility and resources to deliver the experience of them better than anyone else in their category. But the company can't just say "our innovation goal is to evoke the experience of beauty and accomplishment for our customers." It doesn't tell the organization enough to do anything more than scare it. Instead, we need to define what the company will create that when offered will evoke the experience of beauty and accomplishment.

Defining the scope of the experience a company wants to build provides clarity to everyone in the company. By defining the innovation goal in terms of meaning and its associated attributes, the company communicates a shared vision so that all team members, regardless of their function, can see it. Although it's relatively early in the development process, clarifying now what the experience will eventually mean to customers helps coordinate actions and attitudes across the company. It provides a shared starting point for the cross-department collaboration necessary to design an experience that works across multiple touch points.

How detailed this next level needs to be depends in part on the company, its size, and its ambitions. We don't expect a company's innovation process to revolve around a simple phrase, no matter how accurate it may be. But at the same time, it's too early in the process to dictate a fully elaborated design. In our experience, someone (a senior marketing executive, CEO, divisional VP, or a respected consultant) constructs a very brief document or a framework that highlights the central meaning or meanings of the experience and any major factors important to the experience's success. Major factors can include just about anything the company believes is critical, but the most fundamental inclusions are functional value, economic value, emotional value and identity value. These each need to be articulated and related to the overall meaning at this stage in the innovation process

> These each need to be articulated and related to the overall meaning at this stage in the innovation process

Functional value—In layman's terms, this is what "works," the product or service's primary purpose. If the experience model for our shoe company includes functional benefit as a component, it means the functional performance of the shoe will be an important means of delivering the experience and its meaning. Obviously, every product and service needs to function at some level, but emphasizing the functional value in our experience model means it is of critical importance to the meaning of the experience Although functional value is often considered a generic attribute, numerous companies have distinguished themselves through it, including companies like Jiffy Lube, the franchise that promised a ten-minute oil change and QuickBooks, the software from Intuit that automated small business finances,

Economic value—If an experience model includes economic value as a key attribute, it signifies that the meaning of the experience will relate or depend to some extent on financial elements. This could mean the offering will be lower or higher priced than competitive offerings. For example, conveying a meaning of accomplishment or validation sometimes requires pricing the service or product at a premium that prevents all but a select group of customers from buying it, as the American Express Platinum card does by setting a high annual fee. (Alternatively, conveying a meaning of community, as PetSmart does, often requires a more broadly accessible price point.)

Emotional—If an experience model emphasizes emotional benefit, such as excitement, happiness, love, or fear, it indicates the need for sensory stimuli to create a strong feeling state. If our shoe company model accentuates emotional value, then advertising and other means of animating of the offer will be important considerations. For example, if a company wants to emphasize excitement as

Experience framework

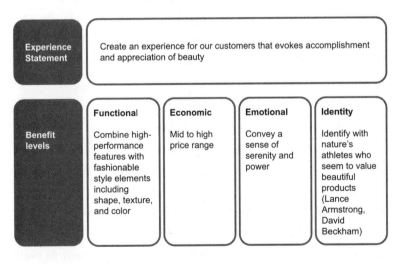

Experience Statement	Create an experience for our customers that evokes accomplishment and appreciation of beauty			
Benefit levels	**Functional**	**Economic**	**Emotional**	**Identity**
	Combine high-performance features with fashionable style elements including shape, texture, and color	Mid to high price range	Convey a sense of serenity and power	Identify with nature's athletes who seem to value beautiful products (Lance Armstrong, David Beckham)

FIGURE 7.1: The experience framework for Footwork, our fictitious shoe company emphasizes meaning that will guide design, outlines the scope of the experience and indicates how the attributes of function, economic value, emotion and identity will be integrated.

an important value of its offering, then Yahoo! is certainly an apt name. Similarly the sense of fun and youthfulness that Pepsi has long represented rests heavily on its identity, its advertising and its promotions.

Identity—If an experience model emphasizes identity, it says that the experience will depend more heavily on the integration of recognized symbols and images tied to specific beliefs and values. The most obvious use of identity are products or services built on celebrity fame, such as Martha Stewart's line of housewares for Kmart or Sean "Diddy" Combs' line of menswear, Sean John. But identity can also reflect imagery and associated qualities of causes, like the Green movement or the religious right; interests, like sailing or fitness; locations, such as the Deep South or the French Riviera and a long list of other options.

An experience framework is not intended to specify direction in detail. Instead, it should be direct and simple enough to fit on one page so it can be pinned to a wall, or propped on a desk. The statement is likely to be revised, so it should be dated, or have a version number. It is not an inviolate declaration, like the Ten Commandments, but rather a starting point that will evolve and grow as the team gains more information, more experience, and more feedback.

Each company department, or function within the innovation team, uses the experience model to guide what it will produce or provide. Strategies and tactics used to realize the vision all derive from this model. If conflicts or confusion arise during the development process, we use the model to mediate them. In fact, every significant step that the innovation team takes should be checked against the goals inherent in the experience model. This process may appear difficult and time-consuming, but adhering to these steps actually speeds development by keeping the team focused on its objectives.

As we've noted, innovation is inherently risky. No amount of planning can fully eliminate that risk, but the likelihood of failure is reduced by carefully framing the experience which the company is committed to produce. By focusing on a clear goal and articulating it for everyone, the shaping and refinement process can proceed. We'll discuss that in the next chapter.

Eight

Shaping the Concept

Having a clearly framed and properly scoped goal of providing a meaningful experience allows the innovation team to shape a concept through an intelligent and deliberate design process, rather than by trial-and-error or free-for-all brainstorming. By following a detailed process and consciously considering all the elements of a new concept from the customer's vantage point, the innovation team creates a clear "blueprint" of what the company should produce or provide. By taking time at this stage to think through all the interrelated aspects of delivering a meaningful experience, a company is less likely to suffer two of the most common failings of experience design: errors of omission and conflicts of intent.

Errors of omission occur when an experience is not executed evenly through all its touch points. For example, when Toyota first introduced its Prius hybrid car, it supplied interested consumers with ample information on its features and benefits, but few of the salespeople in Toyota dealerships understood how the car worked. One of our colleagues went for a test drive, only to have the vehicle run out of gas because the sales representative erroneously thought it could run on battery power alone. This type of omission can be readily identified and prevented at the concept development stage if the innovation team realizes that it's responsible for shaping all dimensions of the experience, not just the product or service.

Conflicts of intent occur when some aspects of an experience actually undermine the desired meaning. A classic example is a fast

food restaurant that emphasizes convenience but doesn't staff ade-
quately, causing customers to line up and wait an excessively long
time. Another example is a luxury pen that is aesthetically beautiful
but doesn't write well. As with errors of omission, conflicts of
intent can be identified and prevented at the concept-development
stage—if the innovation team takes the time to think through all
aspects of the consumer experience.

A truly meaningful experience is consistent throughout all its
dimensions. This goal is more easily realized if the concept is initially shaped in three key dimensions: the breadth of its expression,
the duration of the experience, and the intensity of the customer's
interaction.

Breadth of Expression

Star Trek: The Experience, an attraction owned by Paramount Parks
and located in the Las Vegas Hilton, is an example of how an experience can be built and reinforced through breadth of expression. The
walk-through environment's main offering is an interactive "performance" that mingles a motion simulator, theatrics, special effects,
and the History of the Future Museum. These performances are sur-
rounded and complemented by movie-like sets and live actors
intended to immerse guests in Star Trek author Gene Roddenberry's
vision of the 24th century. Staff members play characters from the
television and film episodes, complete with accurately depicted uniforms, mannerisms, and language. The bar and restaurant are likewise filled with references to characters, locations, and alien species.
Many of the products sold in the stores on the concourse, such as
Romulan Ale and Bajoran jewelry, are straight out of the television
episodes. Even the monorail that delivers guests to the attraction is
themed consistently to evoke the Star Trek experience. Granted, this
is familiar territory for theme parks, with Disneyland being the ear-

liest and most extensive example, but it illustrates the importance of breadth in the design of meaningful experiences.

Using our Footwork example again, let's think about the different ways the experience of beauty and accomplishment can be delivered in the athletic footwear category. Certainly these meanings are expressed through the function and aesthetics of the shoe itself. But what else could be done to extend that experience beyond the product? We might want to extend the meaning of beauty and accomplishment into services, such as guaranteeing the shoe's performance, providing customers a weekly email update of local sports competitions, or offering training advice from experts. We might emphasize the commitment to beauty by selling our shoes only in fashionable stores, or by designing gorgeous shoeboxes and stunning hangtags. When promoting awareness of our shoes, we might show our product in the company of other products that share a similar focus, such as an iPod or Starbucks coffee. The website might include suggestions about matching our shoes to other items of clothing, or it could direct customers to complementary sportswear purchases that fit their color palette or style preference. Our customer support team could be populated with people who have pleasant-sounding voices or with people who are athletes themselves. Our salespeople could be recognized by the attractive but highly functional backpacks they always carry to hold their presentation materials and samples. We could design our offices to be both visually appealing and highly productive. Our spokesperson, maybe even the CEO if appropriate, could be a woman who is both attractive and a top athlete.

By extending the breadth of our concept, Footwork is on its way to delivering the dream of the holistic experience—a company's behavior, offerings and messages integrated to serve customers and provide value at every touch point and in every medium. No company can ensure that 100 percent of its customers experience each dimension consistently; however the conscious

Shaping the breadth of an integrated experience

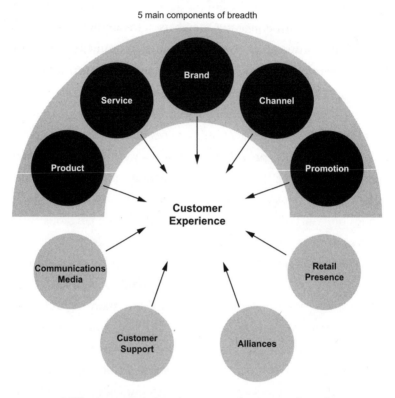

5 main components of breadth

Additional components depend on a company's category and capacity

FIGURE 8.1: An experience is delivered through five components of breadth: product, service, brand, channel, and promotion.

goal of creating an integrated multidimensional experience helps ensure that the final delivery will be as cohesive as possible.

An integrated experience is typically delivered through five main components that comprise the dimension of breadth: product, service, brand, channel, and promotion. Depending on a company's category and capacity, this list could be expanded to include other categories, such as communication media, customer support, alliances, retail presence and more. Carefully considering how the experience is delivered and reinforced by each component helps the innovation team avoid the errors of omission and conflicts of intent. It helps the team explore ways to expand and enrich the experience. Ideally, it prompts members of the innovation team to reexamine consumer understanding gathered from ethnographies or other types of exploratory research for inspiration and guidance in designing each component.

Product

The distinction between products and services is becoming increasingly difficult to define. Here when we talk about product, we're referring to a physical or digital artifact—a "thing" that can be seen, touched, smelled, or heard. Whether that product adds to a meaningful experience depends on careful design, beginning with a clear understanding of the experience the customer desires and proceeding with a deliberate intention to support that specific experience, at least in part, through the product.

Too often, products are created to deliver a function and no serious thought has been given to the customer's experience of using that product. For example, our shoe company's R&D lab might build a model for a shoe that is more comfortable, offers better support, and incorporates a new fabric that repeals mosquitoes. In a typical innovation processes, these features might define the concept simply because they could be presented as "new" and the experience would be an afterthought delegated to marketing. In the process we advocate, however, if the company decided to deliver the experiences of beauty and performance, it would add only those features that support those experiences—in this example, comfort and better support—not the mosquito repellent fabric.

Services

Services are often integrated with products, but unlike products, they are usually dependent on people in some phase of their delivery, and as a result can be more variable. If you think of product as being matter, then services are energy. Both are dimensions of the customer experience, but they operate differently. While Hewlett-Packard can confidently assume that the first printer model it manufactures on any given day will be almost identical to the hundredth produced that day, State Farm Insurance can not be as confident that each of its agents will perform identically.

Although service experiences themselves are often dependent on people, in most cases the service itself involves an interaction with some physical object that can and should be thoughtfully designed. For example, customers experience financial services through products such as checkbooks, websites, and investment tools. Movies are delivered through tickets, seats, screens and popcorn. Even dry-cleaning services are delivered, through vans, hangers and storefronts. As with products, the key to evoking the intended meaning is two-fold: starting with a clear understanding of the experience the customer desires, and developing all the elements of the service to support and contribute to that experience.

Brand

Brand is the expression of an offering's personality. and ideally, it unites all components of a company's offering into an easily recognizable form. Some argue that brand comes before any other component of an experience, including the product or service. Regardless of whether it guides the overall experience or is a contributing part of it, at its best branding is so tightly coupled with the experience design that the connection can't be untangled. Ideally, design interweaves the brand so completely throughout all the components and dimensions that the entire experience is branded.

Brand can guide or control many innovation decisions, including those related to the "look and feel" of the product or service, channel communications, and promotional strategy. For this reason, brand development should always occur simultaneously with product and service development, and all should adhere to the overall experience vision.

The most basic purpose of branding (and harking back to its origins in cattle ranching), is to protect the experience design by declaring its uniqueness and its ownership. A company could try to emulate aspects of the Starbucks experience, but it couldn't copy anything protected by its brand (like its product names or the elements of its visual identity) without risking a serious legal battle. Similarly, when a product or service category approaches commodity status—like banking, gasoline, or basic clothing—brand becomes an important asset in differentiating the experience. Gap has regularly been able to reinvigorate the experience of wearing near-commodity items like white T-shirts and khaki pants through their brand power and influence

Channel

The means by which a product or service is delivered to its consumers is its channel, including all types of retail, direct sales. and online venues. This aspect may seem hard to control for those companies locked into a traditional channel, such as grocery or department stores, where they have little say in how their offerings are sold. For others, channel represents a wide open space, which they can use to complement the customer's experience. Whether a company's channel choices are narrow or broad, its first concern should be ensuring the channel is appropriate for the experience. Our shoe company might typically distribute through REI, the Seattle-based outdoor equipment and clothing retailer. Selling the new model through REI might add to the experience of accomplishment the new shoes are offering. But the rugged, outdoor connotation REI has with most customers might conflict with and thus detract from the experience of beauty. On the other hand, selling the shoe at Nordstrom, or a similar store chain known for its aesthetic taste, is likely to add to the experience of beauty, but would it detract from the experience of performance?

The choice of channel should also be based on the desired buying experience. Each channel—and sometimes each retailer within a channel—differs as to how much customer assistance and advice it provides, what types of facilities and displays it uses, its price range, after-sales support, accessibility, and other aspects that impact a customer's purchase process. The innovation team needs to think through the type of buying process that best supports the experience it's trying to build, and then determine which channels can provide that process.

If the desired channel experience doesn't exist, the innovation team may need to propose and create it. For example, Apple had been selling its computers through chain computer and consumer electronic stores for decades, but these outlets were rarely staffed by personnel who understood Apple products and never offered the kind of experience Apple knew was compatible and complementary with their products. To address this, Apple created its own retail stores. From architecture and materials, to music, to friendly, knowledgeable faces, to customer service, to a range of creative services, to location—by controlling the channel, Apple is able to redefine everything about the shopping experience it offers its customers.

In some cases, the channel itself can be an innovation. CEMEX, a leading global producer and marketer of cement, used existing networks of family and friends to help low-income Mexican families buy homes. The company discovered that communities used their social groups to achieve goals that individuals could not reach. Using this knowledge, CEMEX launched "Patrimonio Hoy," a program that taps into these social groups as a means of providing product information, specialized services, and reasonable financing to a market it previously could not reach.

Promotion

Promotion entails any communication of information about the experience or its related components, including advertising, publicity, sales promotion, merchandising, and direct selling. This is often the most fluid aspect of an experience because it changes so frequently, and it is the most difficult to control—particularly in a global market, where each country has some control over its promotional activities.

While promotion is an extensive topic, we're most concerned here with how potential customers learn of new offerings and how the experience we're building is reinforced through any and all communication and programs, regardless of media or form. In the case of Footworks, this means communications through television, print, and online media, but also include the deals our sales representatives offer, our sponsorship of events, and even the speeches our CEO makes.

A recent promotion by Westin Hotels shows how promotion, as a component of breadth, can support the development of a meaningful experience. In the summer of 2005, an arriving guest would find a small box by his bedside. The front of the package said "Summer reading at Westin—the ultimate in renewal." On the back it read "Books by the pool, books in the heavenly bed, books at the spa." Opening the package, the guest finds an attractive pair of reading glasses. Unlike many cheap or irrelevant products thrown in as a purchase incentive or offered as a complimentary gift, this thoughtfully conceived and beautifully executed promotion was perfectly designed to suit a guest seeking "renewal" and hoping to find that meaningful experience by relaxing with a good book.

Creating breadth of expression using the components of product, service, brand, and more should be a group process, with every member of the innovation team participating. Each component is an important aspect of the final experience, and team members need to understand each other's actions to coordinate their activities across function. For example, at Footwork the better our marketing lead understands the shoes, the more effective she will be in directing the creation of a compelling and appropriate identity for it. The more the sales head knows about the shoe's brand identity, the more precisely he can hone a supporting distribution or launch strategy. And the more the manufacturing manager understands about the sales strategy, the better equipped he is to make intelligent trade-offs on cost and time constraints.

Once an innovation team has considered each component of the experience and determined its breadth, it is ready to move to the next design dimension, duration.

Duration of Experience

Meaningful experiences happen over time. To feel complete, they need a beginning, a middle, and an end. An effective experience design strategy anticipates the unfolding of an experience over time. This could be a simple, linear experience: We view a performance once, enjoy it, and recommend it to others. Other times, it's more iterative: We try a new restaurant, begin to visit it regularly, and become more familiar with it over time. In either case, the design process maps the progression of an experience over time, from initiation through immersion to conclusion and continuation. It then establishes how the experience should spread out across each stage, specifically initiation, immersion, conclusion and continuation.

Initiation
Initiation is the phase when a customer usually encounters one or more of the experiential components (product, service, brand, and so on) for the first time. She notices it and hopefully recognizes at least a suggestion of meaning. Typically, initiation involves an

An Experience Matrix for Footwork

	Product	Service	Brand	Channel	Promotion
Initiation	Visuals in window communicate the meanings of beauty and accomplishment	Consultant for "dressing beautifully for activities" available	Store signage expressing meaning	Walk by new store designed to express meaning	Television celebrity endorsement, limited-time, special consulting available. Ads spread word about brand
Immersion	Shoes worn first week	Consultant shops with customer in Footwork store	Combination of logo on shoes, additional exposure to signage	Additional exposure to store and website	Continuation of above. Perhaps an ongoing series of events
Conclusion	Deep satisfaction meaning evoked	Consultant checks in periodically	Brand now associated with meaning	New visits	End of Series 1
Continuation	Customer buys more	Personalized relationship all about the beauty of the shoes	A broader range of products branded with this symbol of accomplishment and beauty	Store and site constantly evolve as customer perceptions of beauty and accomplishment evolve	Beginning of Series 2, involving more participations with brand

FIGURE 8.2: Design must map the progression of an experience from initiation through immersion to conclusion and continuation.

encounter with the brand through promotion such as reading an ad in a magazine, although it can also be seeing others use the product or service, a chance encounter with a company employee, or mention of the stock performance on the nightly news. For example, some people were introduced to Google, the popular online search company, when a friend recommended, "Just Google it," in response to a question. Others first discovered the company's

services from reading a positive review, hearing about its IPO, or seeing its young, charismatic founders speak at a conference. Still others learned to use the service at work as a means of conducting quick
and easy research.

Since initiation can happen much earlier than a company
intends, an innovation team should consider how its customers
will initially interact with each of the components of an experience.
In our Footwork example, initial customer contact might be when a
person sees the shoes on display and decides to try them on. Initial
contact may be seeing the company and its shoes profiled in a fashion magazine. The first contact might seeing a link that displays the
company's name in a list resulting from a search on the terms "high
performance, beautiful, athletic shoes." Or the initial promotional
contact might be seeing a tiny replica of the new shoe on a girl-
friend's keychain. If an experience is cohesively designed through
the breadth of its components, any initial contact will most likely
do an effective job of representing the company and its offering. At
its best, it will be an enticing sample of the experience and will
attract the people who will most value it

Immersion

The second phase of duration is and immersion, which again
involves interaction with as many of the different experiential components as available. For instance, at Starbucks you experience the
products, services, brand, promotion, and channel, one by one and
in combination throughout the entire visit. Conversely, drinking a
Budweiser at home might just be an experience of the product and
the brand. The more components involved in the immersion phase,
the more avenues a company has for conveying meaning. However,
the more components a company needs to coordinate, the more difficult it is to create and maintain a cohesive experience. In the Budweiser example, only the beer and the package have to coordinate to
deliver the right experience. In the Starbucks example, everything

has to coordinate to deliver the right experience, including the always variable human beings.

Conclusion and Continuation

The third phase of duration is the conclusion, which marks the end of the interaction with the product or service. Conclusion is a state of mind in which the meaning or visceral experience lingers, but our rational mind judges and contrasts it to other offerings or previous experiences. How an experience concludes is critical. because that's what codifies how customers regard the experience and establishes what they expect in the future.

This phase is most evident with experiences that have a finite end to them, such as a hotel stay. Smart hotels treat the check-out process as an integral part of the overall experience. They treat their customer with great respect, thanking her for the visit, providing an appropriate record of the charges. and offering to help with luggage or directions. Less adept hotels under-staff the desk, creating long lines at checkout time, or they slide the closing bill under the guest's door. Maids approach early, anxious to begin cleaning the room for the next person. Bellmen are busy with arriving guests and rush those who are leaving As such, the last impression a customer has quickly turns negative, even if she liked the initial experience and the time she spent at the hotel.

Not every experience should end and not every end is finite. Some experiences, like using an investment service, are continuous, with peaks of higher usage and valleys of lower usage. Other experiences are cyclical, occurring over and over again, such as visiting a restaurant or shopping at a particular store. During each subsequent immersion, the customer's trust in the authenticity of the experience is deepened. Ideally, this provides some insurance against the inevitable breakdown, such as slow service or an out-of-stock problem.

Intensity

In physics, intensity is the measure of energy flow. In design, intensity is a measure of the connection a consumer has with the experience. In experience design, we consider three levels of intensity: reflexive, habitual, and engagement.

The weakest kind of connection is reflexive, more commonly known in marketing as "impulse." A reflex is a nearly unconscious response to stimulus, such as grabbing a tissue to catch a sneeze or filling a glass with ice before adding soda. While companies might want its customers to buy on impulse and reflexively use its products, this happens only in specialized cases. When an impulse buy does occur, it's because the category is highly generic (such as bagged ice), or relatively low-priced with little risk of disappointment (such as gum or candy). Since a reflexive connection can be stimulated in so few product categories and provides little opportunity for experience design, the reflexive level isn't an area of primary concern for us here.

Habitual

We are, however, interested in the habitual level of intensity. A habit is a repeated pattern, behavior, or thought, like how we brush our teeth, tie our shoes, or toss a salad. Habits generally develop from a need for convenience or efficiency, or just from early training. Although these practices are habitual, people are usually willing to modify their behavior for greater convenience, efficiency. or whatever other need gave rise to the habit in the first place. Some habits are built on meaning. Rituals such as serving turkey at Thanksgiving or making the sign of a cross when frightened are a type of habit designed to remind us of greater meaning.

Most companies hope that people will use their offerings in a habitual manner and become loyal customers, but for this to occur and to continue over a sustained period, the products and services typically have to take on deeper meaning. Elephant Pharmacy is a good example of how offering customers a more meaningful experience encourages a more habitual connection. The new Berkeley, California–based drugstore sells everything its customers need from a conventional drugstore, but it also offers a wide selection of alternative health, beauty, and lifestyle products. Its educated staff offers free health and wellness classes and advice on a daily basis, and the store also offers free consultations with a rotating staff of medical experts.

According to CEO and President, Kathi Lentzsch, the experience Elephant Pharmacy seeks to offer its customers is all about "feeling good" and living the good life. "We want customers to come in and not feel rushed to get out, not feel intimidated by what we sell, not feel 'sold to.' The experience is also about choice: We offer customers the opportunity to build on their life and how they choose to live, or we offer them the opportunity to change to a new, healthier way to live—with no judgments on our part." Elephant Pharmacy has consciously designed the shopping experience so that when customers enter the store they feel they *are* living the good life, enjoying an experience of enlightenment and community. This experience keeps them coming back. As Lentzsch explains, "What we hear from people is that they love the feeling of the store. On average, they hang out for 30 to 40 minutes, compared to 5 to 10 minutes in a conventional drugstore." Rather than assuming its customers would habitually return just because the store is conveniently located or offers lower prices, Elephant Pharmacy attracts habitual use by offering its customers a more meaningful experience of shopping.

If an experience has the potential to become habitual, it's worth thinking about how that might be encouraged. Considering our new shoe offering, could we make the shoes feel and look so good that people want to wear them all the time? Can we send customers a daily email message reminding them to workout each day? Could we recommend a weekly shoe cleaning ritual that reminds purchasers of the shoe's performance and beauty? Do we incentivize customers to automatically replace their shoes every six months? These and other reasonable options should be explored by members of the innovation team during the design process.

Engagement

The third level of intensity is engagement. When an experience is engaging, it commands a consumer's conscious attention through nearly all of the stages of duration and the various components of the experience. Many experiences are by their very nature inherently engaging. They might entail risk, like diving off a high platform, or be highly stimulating, like riding a roller coaster. We may be easily engaged by something we find fascinating, like nanotechnology or pictures from the Hubble telescope. Music, art, drama, and other forms of entertainment are successful when they engage the audience emotionally or intellectually. While meaning is not a necessary ingredient of an engaging process (Goliath at Six Flags Magic Mountain doesn't need to deliver meaning to please its stimulation-loving riders), engagement almost always provides an excellent opportunity to convey meaning.

A colleague recently told us about her search for a new car. She made trips to the Subaru, Audi, and BMW dealerships. Each had large, clean showrooms with sales professionals who could articulate their cars' strong points: safety, style, performance, number one ranking in *Consumer Reports*, and so on. In each case, she took a test drive that technically engaged her in driving the car. But in each case, the engagement fell flat. These cars met very high standards, but they remained just cars to her. On a whim, she visited a Mini Cooper dealership and instantly recognized this car-buying experience as different. The environment was hip, stylish, and

informative. Rather than emphasizing the car, Mini Cooper empha-
sized the experience she would have driving the car. For example, a
"Test Drive Accessory" display offered her a variety of music CD's to
play during the drive. Our friend was thrilled to find the Rolling
Stones' "Hot Stuff" among the choices. It didn't take long for her to
realize she was in love with the Mini Cooper. It wasn't how the car
handled, how the seat felt, some vague sense of status associated
with the brand, or the thrill a small car conveys. All these factors
were present and they engaged her. But these attributes were nicely
wrapped in an overall meaning she could only describe as "Hot
stuff." And that's exactly what she wanted in her next car.

Experiences aren't always habitual or engaging; mindlessness
has its virtues, and reflex comes in handy. However, any product or
service category can accommodate development of habitual or
engaged levels of experience—if they're designed appropriately. In
most cases, customers decide the degree of intensity they want. For
instance, in the financial services arena, some people want to be
actively engaged in managing their money. Others want the ease and
efficiency of safe habits. Some people drink a glass of wine as a habitual way to unwind; others savor each sip. Choosing whether to
design for habit or engagement (or somewhere in between these two
levels) means referring back to customer research done in the initial
stage of "Finding Opportunity" and basing that decision on how
those potential consumers you want to reach are likely to behave.

By paying attention to the breadth, duration, and intensity of
the experience as we've outlined here, the innovation team can collectively create a "proof of concept" or early experience prototype
sufficiently detailed to sell the project throughout the organization.
If needed, this early prototype can be shared with trusted partners
or alliances or to elicit consumer feedback. To develop the experience further, the team next moves on to the refinement stage where
the smallest details make a big difference.

Nine

Delivering Reality

B readth, duration, and intensity give shape to an experience, but what guides our interpretation its meaning—what ultimately leads us to decide whether or not we find it personally relevant and fit—are often often much finer details. If the refinments of an experience aren't carefully designed, the experience may seem disjointed, confusing, even false. Unfortunately, this is a common occurrence. A bank will offer to centralize all our financial needs, but then make us use different account numbers, access different websites, and sometimes even visit different branches to experience their promise of unity. A garden-supply company will emphasize the importance of creating a beautiful environment, but package its products in dated, ugly containers. A retailer will expand into a new country and concentrate on the accurate translation of its experience through language, only to offend customers with culturally inappropriate colors, sounds, or smells.

For customers to perceive the meaning of an experience as intended to be clearly perceived, the experience must consistently connect with them. Designing to trigger these critical experiential touchpoints involves primarily two refining dimensions: interactivity between customer and product, and aesthetic details.

Interactivity

Interactivity isn't well understood. To some, it suggests animation. To others, it relates only to "interactive technologies" and devices like computers or Web pages. To still others, it describes a type of action or dialog between two or more people where one response relates to the next. This is a hotly debated topic. Expand the context beyond technology to include the world of consumer goods and services, and the debate becomes even more fragmented.

We see interactivity as the two-way engagement that occurs throughout an experience. The nature of any given interaction lies on a continuum ranging from, on one end, the passive (listening to music on a stereo) and reactive (we see a package on a grocery shelf and react to its message) to the highly interactive on the other, such as responding to a car we see pictured in an ad and then interacting with it on a test drive, or joining Weight Watchers and interacting both in person and online with its counselors and other customers. And there is infinite variety in between.

Of all the possible types and characteristics of interactivity, the ones that interest us most herea re those that most directly contribute to meaning: creativity, productivity, control, adaptability, feedback, and communication.

Control

People expect to have some degree of control over their experiences. This control usually makes them feel more secure, even if it's only illusory, like closing our eyes on a roller coaster. The ability for a customer to control an experience takes many forms. A customer might control the rate of interaction. For example, one customer may drive a car aggressively, pushing its performance to its maximum. Another customer drives the same model more casually, enjoying a different level of interactivity. Another way that customers choose how they will interact is in the sequence of steps they take through the experience. One person may walk down each aisle in a store, while another goes directly to the section she wants. Customers can also exert control over the interactivity of an experience by selecting options they want, such as using only certain features on a microwave or a cell phone and ignoring all the others.

A company can't specifically support every customer's desired level of control, but the innovation team can consider what degree of control most customers will prefer and at what points in the experience. In the case of a film, for example, the expectation of control will be very little; quite the opposite in the case of choosing custom features for a personalized product. This is crucial for experiences that evoke meaning. If a customer feels no level of personal control as the experience unfolds, it's less likely to be meaningful to him.

Adaptability

Experiences that seem to adapt to our interests and behaviors feel more sophisticated and personal. Service components of an experience, particularly those delivered by people, are typically easier to adapt. A childcare provider can continuously adapt to the needs of the children under her care. Adaptations that require change in the product, brand, or channel are more difficult. Our new shoe can't immediately customize its fit to each wearer. The retail store can't easily change the shopping environment to suit each potential buyer. However, if the store's salesperson is talented, she can adapt to each customer and fine-tune the shoe experience for each person she serves.

An experience can seem to be more adaptable if it's designed to change in response to certain conditions. For example, many websites adapt automatically to whether a customer accesses it from one country or region or another, welcoming the customer in a certain language and pre-selecting the content available. Similarly, a service representative may be directed to respond in one of ten

different ways depending on the mood of the caller. Another form
of adaptability is customization. Customization allows customers
to choose options that tailor a product, service, or experience to
their needs and desires. It's typically easier to develop a product
that can be customized than it is to engineer one that can be personalized, since custom options are always finite and controllable
whereas personalized options may be infinite. Personalization
requires a more sophisticated level of interaction and planning, as
choices and options cannot always be anticipated.

Not all customer experience merit the additional time, effort,
and resources needed to be fully personalized. But experiences that
react and respond to participant input have the potential to evoke
meaning more strongly and more personally.

Feedback

An experience that tells us something about itself—that is, that provides information about its status and its response to us—tends to
feel more interactive than one that doesn't. Feedback can be a simple explanation of why we must wait in line, a personal greeting as
we enter pass through a store entrance, or recommended selections
based on a detailed account of our past purchases. Different experiences demand different rates and types of feedback. A video or computer game, for example, provides a great deal of rapid feedback to
the user to keep him engaged and to keep the action progressing.
Relaxing experiences, like stream fishing, typically provide much less
frequent or simpler feedback.

People's expectations of the type and rate of feedback may be
set by their daily routines. When microwaves were introduced, most
women expected them to provide feedback similar to an oven
because that routine was familiar to them. Similarly, skiers often find
snowboarding difficult because they expect the snowboard to
respond to their actions in the way a ski does. When the board's feedback is different, the skier is confused and takes the wrong action.

When an experience is completely new or isn't comparable to a familiar routine, we expect the feedback to at least be coherent, consistent, and observe basic human social conventions. This contention is not new—it's been explored and discussed in the writings of scholars and designers for decades, most notably cognitive scientist Donald Norman, in his book, *Emotional Design* and Stanford professors Cliff Nass and Byron Reeves in their book, *The Media Equation.* We can confirm from our own experience that this expectation of rational and socially appropriate feedback extends to wide classes of products and services, not just technology.

In designing experiences, the team needs to carefully consider the type and rate of feedback needed to support the desired experience. Will Footwork's customers prefer the "spot light" attention given to an athlete or the more reserved, respectful attention given to an artist?

Communication

Experiences that allow customers to communicate, or simply be heard, tend to increase satisfaction. These also allow people to attach meaning to experiences—especially the meanings that are supported by social interactions with others (such as community).

Companies have many options for designing interactive communication within an experience. The simplest approach is to request comments and feedback from customers which many already do. Some firms go even further, regularly updating their customers on the company's plans and seeking their opinions, as Microsoft does in its annual CEO Summit. Amazon's publication of selected customer's "favorites list" and its publication of readers' critiques are examples of communication.

If community is an important element of an experience, then a place where customers can meet, talk, and share personal stories and opinions is vital. In the late 1990's, Nike sought to relate to customers less as a ubiquitous, monolithic corporation and more as a personal, local company. It hired vivid studios, which created interactive experiences for visitors to the Nike website. Vivid focused on connecting custome rs and giving them a voice. The site certainly wasn't the most technologically advanced. On the contrary, it was purposely designed to be compatible with the majority of Web browsers of the time, as well as users with slow, dial-up connections. By focusing on people and building opportunities to hear from its customers, Nike was able to forge new ties with its customers. Nike's strategy today isn't the same, nor should it be; technology and expectations have changed. What hasn't changed, however, is the ability of interactive attributes like control, adaptability, feedback and communication to forge a meaningful two-way connection with customers.

Triggers

We opened this chapter with a discussion of interactivity, but that's not to shortchange the discussion of triggers. In fact, the two-way connection created by an interactive experience is highly dependent on the effective use of aesthetic details, or triggers—the sensory expression of an experience.

In the early 1940's, Louis Cheskin was hired by a restaurant chain in Chicago that needed to increase its revenue. Louis visited one of the restaurants and noted a large sign on the roof announcing "Hot Food" (remember, this was the early 1940's). His subsequent report to the chain owner instructed the company to change the color of the roof from blue to red before considering any other revisions to the menu, restaurant design, or advertising. The owner made the change and sales jumped 30 percent within the first few months.

This anecdote, although decades old, remains an excellent example of the impact of triggers. The restaurant changed nothing but the color of the roof, but that one modification dramatically changed customers' opinion of the restaurant.

Getting the sensory details, like the color, of an experience right is important because it's often these details that create first impressions and evoke an initial sense of meaning. These fine points become code that a customer will interpret quickly and use to measure her interest.

The role of triggers was a primary focus of Louis Cheskin's work in the 1930s and 1940s. It was then that he first discovered a trait he called "sensation transference," in which the aesthetic properties of a package directly influences a customer's experience of a product or service. Cheskin now has literally thousands of case studies documenting the power of triggers. While most examples focus on visual triggers, it's well known that non-visual sensory triggers have the same power. For example, in the 1980's MIT's Media Lab conducted tests of high-definition television prototypes. The researchers put two different prototypes next to each other and asked people to judge which had the better picture. In one test, the screens were identical—the prototypes differed only in the quality of the audio. Despite these identical screens, people consistently claimed that the system with the better sound quality had a better picture. In this case, the higher quality of the sound influenced people's perception of the picture.

Triggers can instantly—but often subconsciously— evoke an element of meaning and as such, they are valuable assets to an innovation team. The most common triggers available to designers and marketers are language, symbols, and sensations.

Language

Words are obviously important in conveying information, instruction, and details throughout all the components of an experience. With the exception of the "artist formerly known as Prince," most brands are recognized not by their logos alone but by their names or their abbreviations (even Prince now recognizes the need for a name). While there are many effective ways to create a powerful brand name, brands built on words that directly represent the experience offered, like Air France, *Fast Company* or *Country Life*, will help form the customer's perception of the experience. By using language that in its cadence and tone embodies the broader experience it supports, words can deliver meaning beyond their literal value. Exclamations like "Pow!" and "Bam!" in a Batman movie contribute to a viewer's sense of excitement, while military euphemisms such as "collateral damage" or "surgical accuracy" recast the chaotic experience of war as a controllable event.

Technically, words *are* symbols—the letters represent sounds that our cultures teach us to recognize as indicating particular objects, concepts, or phenomena—but in most cases, words are able communicate shared meaning more precisely than a graphic symbol. Although software programs offer symbol-only menus to conserve screen space, most users find simple words like "search" and "favorites" faster and easier to recognize than a magnifying glass and a star.

Unfortunately, words and phrases are rarely universal, even among people with a shared language. A word can have numerous associations or connotations, depending on the speaker's region, age, gender, occupation, education level, and more. This makes words difficult to use in designing globally applicable experiences. Unless key terms are carefully translated into a customer's language, they will become ineffective communicators at best and misleading at worst.

Symbols

A symbol is an artifact that represents a concept or a quality. Unlike words, a symbol usually enjoys relatively consistent interpretation, at least within its originating culture and in some cases, internationally. For example, an arrow is universally understood to indicate direction. A symbol can be a direct reflection of its meaning, such as a plus sign signifying "added" or "more," or a stylized or allegorical version with less obvious ties, like a horseshoe representing luck. In the case of brand logos, symbols can be invented and attain meaning over time, like the "swoosh" now universally associated with Nike or the curved bottle that has become synonymous with Coca-Cola. But when symbols are created or used for various purposes, an innovation team and its designers need to ensure their customers interpret the symbol's meaning as the company intends. A heart means love in many contexts, but to those watching their cholesterol, a heart on a food product label or a menu indicates a low-fat entree.

Although we tend to think of symbols as design elements, other sensory elements can be symbolic as well, making them powerful conveyors of meaning in the design of an experience. The sound of a Harley-Davidson has become symbolic of its performance. A new-car smell is synonymous with a vehicle fresh off the production line. The ultra-soft feel of mink, silk, or fine leather is a symbol of luxury.

Sensations

Without their acquired meaning, the noise from a motorcycle and the smell of a new car would just be sensations. Sensations refer to what consumers can perceive through sight, sound, smell, taste or touch. (Some might argue for another dimension that accounts for a mental or psychic "vibe," but we'll leave that for another book.). The palette of sensations a designer can use to refine experiences is extraordinarily rich. It includes color, hue, shape, texture, music, rhythm, aroma, vibration, and anything else our senses can perceive and distinguish. These elements are commonly used in product and brand design but can just as easily add dimension to service offerings, environments, and promotional activities. Nordstrom's practice of employing a pianist to provide customers with live music is an element of sound added to the environment. A masseuse's use of aromatherapy adds an element of smell to the service of massage.

The interpretation of a sensation is often subjective. This can make it difficult to choose a sensation that is appropriate to the meaning a company is trying to evoke. For example, the color white evokes freshness and renewal in much of the world, but in China, it is associated with sadness and mourning. A rural listener might hear the sound of running water and infer a stream nearby, where an urban listener concludes there's a broken water main. The smell of incense may have religious connotations to some, while some Baby Boomers associate it with smoking pot in the 1960's.

Ideally, if a word, symbol or sensation is well integrated into an experience, it can become emblematic of its meaning, communicating intent quickly and convincingly. For many of its customers, a faint whiff of McDonald's French fries brings to mind the entire experience of visiting the quick-serve restaurant and all its connotations, both good and bad. Because they tend to operate at an almost instinctive level, these triggers, once activated, are extremely difficult to revise or undo. It's a wise innovation team that invests upfront to thoroughly understand a trigger's implication before incorporating it into an experience.

Confirming Perceptions

While it's tempting for experience developers to assume they know the value of triggers, or can create a new trigger and imbue it with meaning, that's a risky and potentially costly proposition.

Without confirming customers' perception of triggers, it is easy for companies to inadvertently create misleading or confusing expressions of meaning—or worse—offend their customers at the social level rather than connecting with them at the level of meaning. For example, within our own culture, we're so accustomed to the symbolic meanings of color—white for purity, red for passion, blue for calm—that we don't recognize that these meanings are not universal.

In 2004, Cheskin collaborated with MSI-ITM and CMCD Visual Symbols Library on a study of color. Thanks to the speed of the Internet, we were able to survey nearly 13,000 people in 17 countries over a few weeks to learn what different colors meant in different contexts. We first asked respondents to pick a favorite color, and then continued by focusing on eight colors (red, blue, green, purple, orange, yellow, black, and white) asking participants to rate the colors in terms of their association with certain attributes, products, companies, and countries.

While it's tempting for those charged with experience developers to assume they know the value of triggers, or can create a new trigger and imbue it with meaning, that's a risky and potentially costly proposition.

Among many intriguing findings, the study confirmed that perceptions of color differ significantly by culture. While blue is a global favorite, some countries next choice is red but others choose purple, green, or black. Red is the universal color of love, but in Asian countries, orange has the second highest love connection. In English-speaking countries, purple is the romantic runner-up, while in Brazil, Mexico, and France, white speaks of romance. Yellow nearly equals red's heat in Spain. Needless to say, our athletic shoe company has much to consider in deciding the color of its brand identity if it seeks a market beyond the U.S.

Perhaps the most complex and vexing part of understanding triggers is their tendency to change. Because we live in an increasingly multicultural environment with the opportunity for ideas, concepts and beliefs to cross-pollinate, the triggers we produce and respond to are not as codified as they were in the past. If we think about the range of tastes that trigger love and connectedness in our extended family, we may well find that each generation identifies a completely different sensation. For our parent's generation, it might include the familiar taste of chopped liver, meatloaf, or a tuna casserole. For us, it might be the sweetness of Mrs. Fields cookies.

> Perhaps the most complex and vexing part of understanding triggers is their tendency to change.

For our nieces and nephews, it may be the pure flavor of organic vegetables and tofu stir-fry. The demand for the meaningful experience stays the same, but the effective triggers evolve. This type of change can be ascertained through traditional research methods on an "as needed" basis, but we have long advocated the importance of maintaining a current and accurately defined vocabulary of triggers.

A vocabulary of triggers can be created through a combination of ethnographic work and quantitative surveys that are longitudinal—that is, repeated over time. This mix combines the ability of ethnography to identify the nuances of cultural distinctions with the ability of quantitative metrics to measure the size and significance of change. This approach is not as complicated as it may seem, if we observe a few guidelines:

1. Hire trained, professional ethnographers to identify the most salient and triggers in each culture that are relevant to the type of experiences a company provides. Anthropologists with graduate-level training and commercial ethnography experience typically have an acute sensitivity to working in unfamiliar cultural contexts and can recognize triggers that others wouldn't see. Ethnographers who are of the culture being studied are the most attuned its distinctions.

2. Choose locations carefully. Unless the country's culture is homogenous (and few are), the choice of location for ethnographic observations can greatly skew the results. Using the U.S. as an example, imagine if an ethnographer reported back on the country's most important triggers after conducting a dozen ethnographies only in Hawaii (leis would certainly be included). Locations should be selected to ensure that they don't under- or over-represent characteristics that are not common to the population being studied.

3. Capture the essence of the trigger. This may seem obvious, but ethnographers sometimes think everything can be reduced to words. Photographs and audio recordings are often much easier to understand than written descriptions. Similarly, whenever possible, the ethnographers should bring back real examples.

4. Create a central archive. A central archive of triggers eases access and ensures cohesive application across cultures. Current technology tools make this a relatively simple task to accomplish, particularly the visual databases, virtual shared collaboration spaces, mobile computing tools, and digital photography.

5. Monitor the attributes and meanings associated with key triggers. Establishing a baseline understanding of what triggers imply to people and updating this periodically helps design teams use words, symbols and sensations accurately across cultures and over time. Watch for changes, and don't assume a small change is insignificant. Big shifts all have a starting point.

Taking the time to fully investigate the cultural significance of triggers and their power to refine the details of an experience creates a reusable asset for the innovation team that moderates risk and increases the likelihood of success. Used properly, a vocabulary of triggers (or if that's not feasible, ad hoc feedback on selected triggers) can improve the design of the product or service. It can ensure that the experience is accurately understood and interpreted, and clarify the communication of meaning throughout the experience.

The ultimate goal of an experience design team is this meaningful, two-way connection with customers. Developing the right triggers and elements of interactivity initiates this connection and fosters its growth. Once these refining details are envisioned, the innovation process can shift from development to execution (assuming the company approves going forward at this point) and we can tackle the final . phase in delivering meaningful experiences; that of sustaining it over time and helping it evolve. We'll turn to that next.

Ten

The End in Sight

Implementing an experience is always messier than planning one. As the process moves from whiteboards, computer screens, and paper, into concrete action it's more difficult to control and can at times verge on chaotic. As challenging as it was for the innovation team to consider and plot all the various factors that would evoke desired meanings, it's that much more difficult to now make that plan a reality. This final phase of delivering meaningful experiences requires the entire company to act in concert.

The details of final production vary widely from company to company. We can't possibly address the myriad processes, checkpoints, actions, and approval rounds each company navigates when turning a plan into reality, but we can explain the unique twists that implementing meaningful experiences adds to this final phase of the innovation process. For one thing, it's non-linear, which means it's the opposite of an assembly-line process. When we think of an assembly line, most of us envision a large, well-organized manufacturing facility where parts are added together in a step-by-step process. The car or candy or T-shirt progresses down the line, acquiring parts at designated stations, until it's finally complete, ready to be shipped to awaiting stores. Even with the most complex product, with thousands of parts and hundreds of inspection points, the process remains time-ordered with discrete steps. The same can not be said of the production of customer experiences—particularly ones that seek to convey a compelling sense of meaning.

The actual implementation of an experience-design plan is a process characterized by a network of interconnected and overlapping decisions. Using our shoe company example, manufacturing might be working from prototypes that are still being influenced by design or marketing. The ad agency might be designing the website while the sales team is still debating which countries should be covered in the launch. A potential retailer might be adding the shoe to its upcoming catalog while the finance is reviewing the price. There's no streamlined hand-off from one station to the next. Instead, production takes shape more like a movie with a loose script, a lot of actors, and the innovation team playing the director.

In this directing role, the innovation team members are often the only ones in a position to ensure that deadlines and tradeoffs don't erode or alter the desired meaning, and that everyone in the company is trained to convey and support that goal. These are daunting tasks. It takes tenacity to maintain the integrity of an experience's meaning in the face of deadline pressures, cost-cutting mandates, aggressive sales managers, hungry Wall Street analysts, enthusiastic PR agents, and a host of other influences that may inadvertently make decisions that negatively impact the experience.

Here's an example of how last-minute decisions can derail the innovation team's efforts. Cheskin once worked with a client that created a new technology designed to help users work more efficiently and also feel a stronger sense of accomplishment. Throughout the planning process, everyone collaborated with the core meaning of "accomplishment" as the guiding vision. The plans for the product design, the branding elements, the sales support, merchandising—every element of the experience reinforced that meaning. Then, just as the production phase started, the VP of marketing got excited by a new branding idea from the ad agency and tossed out the previously approved name, positioning and packaging, reasoning that the new identity was more exciting and unique. Unfortunately, the new branding did not convey "accomplishment" and was inconsistent with all the other elements of the experience the company was trying to create. While the brand identity was novel, it ended up confusing consumers because it did not relate to or support the experience of accomplishment. This may seem like a minor detail, but it's the equivalent of a movie producer deciding to change the title of his serious drama to "The Adventures of Furry Bunny" because it will appeal to a broader audience.

As we've stressed in our discussion of the phases of the innovation process, to effectively convey meaning, an experience needs to be consistent, and consistency comes from a shared vision that everyone in the company supports. Although it may be uncomfortable for the innovation team to play the role of enforcer, it has to keep this type of last-minute disruption to a minimum. The only way we know of to do this is by asserting authority through regular check-in meetings, clear communications, and some degree of group decision-making. It's never easy, but this approach can manage creative chaos. The innovation team's efforts can be further facilitated if their collaborative spirit and customer focus is encouraged to spread throughout the company.

That spirit of collaboration and shared customer focus are also essential to managing another twist that gets introduced at the implementation phase, namely this: If you're successful at delivering a meaningful experience, the production process really never ends.

Perpetual Production

Meaningful experiences are not widgets that a company ships to warehouses to be dispatched as needed, or a fixed set of services that its employees provide to customers. They emerge as part of the connection a customer makes with a company through the use of its products, services, brands, distribution channels, communications, and any other related outreach. This connection continues beyond the initial exposure or use, and it continues to be shaped and influenced by the company's actions.

One apt example is BP, formerly known as British Petroleum. Oil is one of few industries that normally looks ahead 30 years in its planning process, and as a result, is not usually known for radical change. Under the leadership of CEO John Browne, however, BP looked into the future and saw the need to do something completely different. Rather that continue to think of BP as an oil company, the company saw a future of new technologies, including alternative fuels and cleaner means of using traditional fuels. So it recast itself as an energy company, one that was open to exploring anything that might entail.

Naturally, this change in focus called for a new brand identity; BP now stands for "Beyond Petroleum." But the new face reflects fundamental changes in the way bp approaches innovation. No longer satisfied evoking only accomplishment, the company introduced duty, community, and even harmony to its core meanings. The company's commitment to the new message is apparent to the financial community in the investments, acquisitions, and hires BP has made. To its customers, the message is clear in its advertising and marketing.

The Experiential Company

This continual need to substantiate a meaningful experience is an important consideration for any company. Unfortunately, the maintenance phase of an experience and its ongoing evolution is something innovation teams often overlook, but they can play an important role in ensuring that it happens. Delivering a relevant, authentic, and ultimately meaningful customer experience requires that everyone in the company adopt a mindset that is experientially oriented, regardless of an employee's title or position. When everyone becomes an experience designer—in terms of thinking about, participating in, or delivering meaningful experiences to their customers—the likelihood of success rises exponentially. Creating and maintaining this mindset helps ensure that a customer encounters a consistent, comprehensive experience whether he is trying on a shoe, calling the company for information, or visiting its website. The most effective means we've found of doing this are through training, continual communication, and consumer champions.

> When everyone becomes an experience designer—in terms of thinking about, participating in, or delivering meaningful experiences to their customers—the likelihood of success rises exponentially

Training employees to support and contribute to the customer experience may seem like a "no-brainer" that every firm does, but it's surprising how few companies invest in this type of training, and when they do, how superficial that training frequently is. Typically, employees are trained to address complaints, to offer customers assistance in selecting among products or services, and perhaps even to make friendly small talk. But few companies take the time and effort to immerse their employees in the customer's experience and what it means. Even fewer educate their employees on how each can help convey, sustain, and enhance that experience.

In 2003, Levi's found an excellent way to provide this type of training to its employees through a process called Immersion Clinics. The popular clothing retailer asked over a hundred of its managers and directors to devote a day to getting in-depth insights into how its customers think and behave. Working with Levi's Consumer Insights team, Cheskin spent several months observing,

interviewing, and recording people about their experience of clothing, jeans, and Levi's. With the resulting footage and knowledge, we
constructed a walk-through exhibit that allowed 30 to 40 people at
a time to surround themselves with views of consumer life, including videos of individual customers talking about what clothing
meant to them; "shrines" that displayed popular clothing, accessories, media, and memorabilia for six different sorts of people; a
website that provided details on specific types of customers and
what they wanted; and a variety of colorful posters, journals and
other portable reminders of what each participant learned during
the day's activities. After spending time in the immersion space,
executives gathered in work sessions to discuss and debate the
meanings that Levi's customers' value, and how the company could
improve customers' experience of their products, services, and
brand.

Maintaining the Mindset

This type of training is an excellent starting point, but maintaining
an experiential mindset throughout a company also requires constant communication of relevant information, such as regular
updates on customers' requests, comments, and reactions. This kind
of informative feedback helps to orient the company's culture and
keep it focused on the customer experience. Keeping this type of
information flowing throughout the organization also reminds
employees that the company values pleasing customers as a continual process, rather than as something to be pursued for a defined
period or through some specific action.

Both virtual environments, like intranet sites or in-house
knowledge- management systems, and physical environments like
hallways and lobbies can offer powerful aids to company-wide
learning. Microsoft has invested significant time and effort to

develop internal websites that help any of its 25,000 employees better understand consumers around the world. Visit any lobby on the vast Redmond campus, and you are likely to see life-sized posters of customers with real quotes about their experience of using Windows, Office, Xbox, or any other product or service the company is launching or updating. Placing these visual reminders at "crossroads" within company offices creates a presence that permeates all levels of an organization and provides a constant reminder that customers are real people, not abstract sales data, making their concerns and desires easier to understand and address.

Another mechanism to help an organization stay focused on the customer's experience is to designate a "consumer champion"—an employee whose role is to advocate for the customer's point of view. He or she acts on behalf of consumers (both current customers and potential ones), voicing their responses to proposed ideas or iterations, and guiding company behavior. Unlike a market or design researcher who may only provide information, the person holding this position should have the authority and personal characteristics to influence the design of experiences. Authority comes from top management creating this role and supporting the person who fills it, but choosing someone with the right character traits is every bit as important. One designer we know refers to this role as "Rambo," a comment on the persistence and resiliency the consumer champion needs. We don't actually think this is a combat position, but it does take a particular type of background and dedication to understand what consumers need from a company and to fight for that outcome. The ideal consumer champion embodies these three traits: knowledge, empathy, and focus.

To be effective, a consumer advocate needs to have current and comprehensive knowledge of those aspects of people's lives that are relevant to the experience. In our shoe company example, this advocate should understand a consumer's perspective and behavior around clothing, shoes, athletic performance, and style.

He needs to assimilate this information and develop an intuitive sense of how people will react to decisions the innovation team makes. Even the most customer-centric organizations can not afford to test every decision they make. A knowledgeable consumer advocate can guide the hundreds of smaller decisions that are important but don't merit a full-scale study. For example, one company we worked with in the late 1990's was introducing a radically new technology. Their consumer advocate asked the product developers to pretend to be customers and act out how they would use the product. The consumer advocate helped each developer stay in character and accurately portray a consumer's behavior. This improvisation helped everyone on the team realize the significance of many fine design details they may have otherwise overlooked—details that conveyed meaning.

Another important trait of a consumer champion is empathy. Empathy, or the ability to "put oneself into another's shoes," tends to be a trait a person either does or does not have; it's not something easily taught. A consumer champion who is empathetic can provide a more humanistic perspective than market data alone. For example, based on his empathy for consumers, our shoe company consumer advocate might counsel the innovation team against developing too many style options, arguing that while people have specific preferences, they also want the company to be confident in its expression of style. This interpretive perspective is hard—sometimes impossible—to get directly from customers.

The final trait we look for in a consumer champion is focus. Anyone in this position should have just one goal to focus on: ensuring that customers are pleased with the experience. To be effective in this, he can't afford to factor in other considerations like financial performance or channel limitations. He shouldn't expect to win every battle but needs to let the innovation team, and the company at large, know when it is doing something that might compromise the company's relationship with its customers.

Tracking the Future

Because providing a meaningful experience is an ongoing process that evolves over time, tracking consumers' reaction to it gives feedback on the company's current performance and its future direction. This kind of evaluation isn't new to companies, but it's usually too narrow in its focus and it's rarely integrated into the development process. A typical post-launch tracking study measures how many people bought a product or service, where they bought it, and for what purpose. Some will track attributes that are associated with the brand (such as "is high quality" or "is a leader in the category"), checking every six to twelve months to see how they change relative to competitors and other market dynamics. Still others may solicit ideas on how the company can improve its offerings and what else it could provide. This is all valuable information, but to be useful to innovation teams looking forward, it needs more depth and detail.

For example, a standard evaluation of our shoe company's offerings might show that 10 percent of our target market bought the shoes in the first six months after launch, primarily through department stores and as a complement to casual attire. We learn that customers associate our brand with the attributes of "fresh style" and "beautiful," but less so with "powerful" or "helps me reach my goals." A few customers comment that the price should be lowered in the future.

When we probe further beyond where a traditional tracking study would go, customers explain that the experience of beauty is immediate, but performance and the resulting sense of accomplishment take time, particularly since they don't usually think of these two qualities as being compatible. They also explain that if the shoes actually deliver on both, they will be worth the price. They offer ideas on how to convey this meaning better, including endorsements from leading athletes, sponsorship of "extreme" sports events like the X Games, and more visible performance features in the shoes. This is information the innovation team can use.

This richer evaluation is readily available, but to be believable and powerful enough to enact change, feedback needs to come through the interactions of employees with customers, not just through the market research department.

A company's leaders should meet its customers as often as possible, at the very least a few times a year. This may seem obvious, but how often is it put in practice? In smaller companies, it is generally inevitable that the executives meet the customers. However, in major corporations senior executives are often insulated from their customers by layers of management, procedure, or their own lifestyles. A couple of years ago, we met with the head of large conglomerate whose companies were interested in developing more products for teenagers and young adults. This executive was proudly recounting how he felt in touch with this segment of the market because his country club had several teen members. He explained that the most avant garde of these teens were males who pierced their ears, and he suggested this was a new trend that would soon sweep the nation. We had to gently reveal to him that, far from being trendsetters, these young men were actually late in adopting a fad that had already gone mainstream years before. Since the only teens he met were the sons of wealthy, conservative families, his view of that population was very narrow.

We've all heard similar stories about automobile executives who don't have to maintain their own cars, airline executives who don't regularly fly economy class, or food industry executives who don't cook. But many executives take seriously, and rightly so, the need to put themselves in the place of their customers in order to understand what they need—and how well their company is meeting those needs. These executives realize it's simply bad business to be misinformed about the world and the markets they serve. In some cases, they take over for briefly for employees with direct customer contact, manning a cash register in a retail outlet, or answering customer calls on a support line. Sponsoring and attending community events offers valuable opportunities for management to meet customers and find out how people actually experience their offerings.

Managers more frequently go out of their way to immerse themselves in their own companies' experiences, but surprisingly few make the same effort to check up on the competition. The American auto industry was notorious for ignoring foreign competitors' offerings and suggesting employees should drive only company-built cars. Similarly, we've had clients who were adamant that we never use competitor's products, suggesting this was a sign of disrespect or lack of loyalty. On the contrary, a regular practice of experiencing a competitor's offerings gives an executive a point of comparison that's usually much more revealing than the standard competitive intelligence report.

In addition to executive contact with customers and competitors, employees throughout an organization are often party to first-hand feedback from customers on their experiences. These responses can be very valuable if acquired systematically and interpreted accurately. If employees have been trained and educated to understand the experience their company is seeking to convey, and if see themselves to be a valued part of that delivery, they are far more capable of accurately assessing its success or failure with customers. If they are able to relay these assessments to a central authority (the consumer champion is a good choice) in an easy and standardized way, their individual reports can be aggregated and take on much greater worth.

This function should not be confused with customer support centers. In most cases, personnel in the customer support department deal with complaints and problems. It's a rare person who calls customer service to talk about how much she enjoys the details of an experience or to offer ways it can be enhanced. If a customer needs to call customer support, she is usually already a little annoyed and doesn't necessarily reflect the market as a whole.

A Second Opinion

Our recommendation that employees and executives seeking regular and direct feedback from their customers doesn't mean a company should replace the role of researchers. The same sort of approaches, questions, and measures we described earlier for exploring the market as a whole should also be employed to provide the innovation team with feedback after a launch. Ethnographies, particularly if they are done by professionals who have a broad view of consumer lifestyles, can help companies understand how their current customers are evolving and what impact this will have on their experience of the company's product, services, and brand. Often the most important insights come from a company learning that its customers' need for meaning is evolving away from what the company conveys. This is easy to see in retrospect. Customers valued large, powerful cars until the gas crisis of the early 1970's prompted many to value smaller, efficient ones that connected with the environmental movement and its meaning. The experience of unity, reinforced by campaigns like the "Pepsi Generation" and Coke's "I'd Like to Teach the World to Sing" was replaced with the experience of freedom consumers felt experimenting with countless versions of teas, juices, waters, and even colas. Nearly every industry or market has its history of disruption driven by customers changing the meaning they value. The trick is to see it coming.

Firms with vast customer information databases can detect trends in mass consumption. Companies will "mine" the data, going beyond the simple measure of what people wanted yesterday to look for purchasing and interaction patterns that might suggest emerging needs and preferences. While data mining can sense potentially significant trends, it has one key limitation: it can't determine the types of experiences people seek. It can point out the trend, but it rarely reveals the underlying motivation behind all of the data or the other influences shaping and modifying customers' perception. Consequently, effective data mining should be seen as an early-warning mechanism that can detect subtle signals of change which then should be investigated. Ideally, this investigation will use ethnographic techniques and will be done in partnership with a firm that has a broader perspective on consumer experience than any one company. With this broader and deeper view, a firm and its innovation team can learn what how and why desired meanings are evolving early enough to avoid its own extinction.

Eleven

Moving Forward

I s "making meaning" just a fleeting fashion? An idea suited to 2006 and maybe a year to two beyond but destined to fade as soon as the next fresh idea hits the market? We don't think so. We have traced its roots and see it as a logical and timely evolution. It incorporates the functional and economic emphasis of the early 1900's, and it grows comfortably out of the focus on emotion and identity that characterized the last half of the 20th century.

Our belief in the validity and viability of this business strategy also stems from our conversations with business leaders. Most have exhausted the benefits of earlier approaches and are investigating new approaches. More often than not, when they explain what is missing from their current innovation practices, the lack centers around the need for a deeper understanding of customers, a less linear, more collaborative practice, and a heightened sensitivity to the power of design.

For businesses, the benefits of adopting an innovation process that focuses its efforts on the delivery of meaningful experiences are many. First and foremost, it offers a new avenue for creativity and a new manner for a company to distinguish itself. Line extensions or brand remakes can become more expansive and significant, going beyond a simple upgrade or a new flavor. Products and services can better complement each other and leverage other components like distribution channels, promotional activities and brand to strengthen a company's overall offering.

An emphasis on meaningful experiences also offers new means for a company to add value to existing customer relationships and make those relationships more stable and enduring. Rather than constantly fighting to keep customers through price cuts or the addition of new features, a company can gain a more protected position within its customers' lives—a position that promotes growth.

By adopting a design process that emphasizes a customer focus and that intentionally integrates all aspects of an experience, innovation teams can orchestrate collaboration in a way that benefits customers, employees, and their company as a whole. By moving beyond the product-and-engineering focus of Six Sigma, companies can realign their approach to innovation so that it is initiated by customers' needs and desires, rather than the company's capabilities. Finally, by acknowledging the importance of detail and the power of aesthetics in every point of contact and each interaction, companies will be able to speak in a language that is comprehensible to customers worldwide.

Meaningful experiences add value because they touch on ideals and beliefs we holds dear, but they do more than this. Because a meaningful experience depends on repeated, consistent delivery, it typically engenders greater trust. As customers' trust in a company deepens, their loyalty becomes stronger. They adopt a more informal relationship with the company, one that eases transactions on both sides, making them faster, better and more predictable.

In the coming years, we expect a growing percentage of people to shift their consumption toward more meaningful transactions. Whether they are fulfilling a desire to live a more harmonious life filled with yoga, meditation and organic food or to be awed by the magic of science and technology, today's leading-edge consumers of meaningful experiences are important to watch because they represent the future.

What's the Future?

As with all market evolutions, not everyone will modify his or her buying habits, nor will all businesses be prompted to change. We're reasonably sure a backlash movement will arise arguing against business developing along these lines, seeing it as an invasion of territory reserved for religious or non-commercial entities. Some forms of backlash already exist. Movements such as anti-globalization activism or the "No Logo" faction reflect heartfelt frustration with businesses that treat people like commoditized consumers instead of respecting them as individuals. This type of reaction against "branded meanings" is understandable, but we believe these critics have it backwards. A company that pursues innovation to deliver meaningful experiences is not trying to dominate or "own" a category of meaning. Instead, it is trying to make it possible for people to more easily access the experience of a particular meaning. To do more than this would be improbable, if not impossible. Nevertheless, some will be uneasy with commercial firms entering this realm, claiming it to be the exclusive domain of more traditional sources of meaning.

But let us leave aside the debate over the appropriateness of this approach. If, as we predict, we start to see a proliferation of meaningful customer experiences, what does that mean to us in terms of how we live and the work we do as business leaders?

Kinder, Gentler Corporations? Will this movement reform business and make every organization who adopts it more caring and sensitive? No, it won't. This is not a reform movement striving to improve work conditions or to replace capitalist practices with social conventions. This is movement emerging from informed purchasers who are using their increasing commercial power and control to obtain what they want from companies. To the extent that businesses respond and meet that demand, they may become more sensitive to their customer's view of reality, but that doesn't mean a company will be any less ambitious or any less aggressive in devising its business strategies.

Monolithic Market Leaders? Whenever a company gains dominant power it runs the risk of being identified as a juggernaut, feared and resented for its tendency to trample smaller cultures and wipe out entrepreneurs; to resist such dominance seems futile. If large businesses begin to align their innovation strategy more demonstrably with meaning as an approach to growth and expansion, will they impose their dominance on the customers as well, insisting that they accept certain types of meaning? Fortunately, we think that's very unlikely. Most companies are not really interested in changing human behavior or popular culture as their primary goal; that path is fraught with risk and far too expensive. Instead, most are simply interested in following culture's lead and leveraging the opportunities provided by change.

Although the benefits to business are many, the true leaders and ultimate beneficiaries in this evolution are customers—customers who are starting to sense and use the power they have to participate in the process of innovation and to influence its outcome. By identifying the experiences they value and rewarding those companies that provide them, customers are the real design directors. They are ones deciding what feels right, and what seems faked. They are the one's deciding what triggers mean, which mediums are most effective, what level of intensity works, if the duration is sufficient, and whether the components of the customer experience are consistent and integrated. There's little risk of companies becoming totalitarian when it is their customers who have the real power.

Consumer Dictators? Does this mean consumers will be able to dictate to business, becoming tyrants of individual demand? There's a kernel of truth to this prediction: we do see customers' power increasing as the demand for meaningful experiences grows.

But like the fear of the market monolith, this scenario is exaggerated. The real threat consumers always pose to business is to withdraw their demand completely. That's why The Conference Board tracks the Index of Consumer Confidence and why a decline in confidence is considered bad for the economy. But that collective power to depress the economy is not the same as an individual expressing dissatisfaction with a company by shifting loyalty to another competitor.

To please customers and connect with them in an authentic, believable way, a company will need a very clear view of what people want and need in their lives, and an honest assessment of which of these desires it can really serve. Over-promising a product's capabilities or a service's uniqueness is regrettable, but customers often excuse such behavior, even expect it. We know that blindingly fast computer will seem slower than we expect. We know even FedEx might occasionally miss a delivery date. Most people have learned not to expect perfection from businesses. But a lack of perfection may not be as excusable in the realm of meaningful experiences. If our shoe company claims its primary commitment is to our sense of beauty and accomplishment, but then supplies shoes that are out of style or technically inadequate in their performance, it's not easy to excuse this as predictable slip-up. We're much more likely to interpret it as ignorance, incompetence, or deceit.

Consumer Utopia? Will the availability of more meaningful experiences expressed through a wider variety of products, services, brands, retailers, and the like make us happier? We can envision that if we can substitute superficial experiences with more meaningful ones, we may feel more satisfied, but ironically, increased happiness doesn't necessarily follow.

Historically, a market develops to meet existing demand, but it also creates new demand as consumers become aware of new options. A person thinks she's satisfied with a car, only to hanker for a different one a month later. A family enjoys its first cruise, but later learns of a larger ship with better activities. This "paradox of choice" is a normal response, according to Barry Schwartz, a Swarthmore professor and author of numerous books on human nature. The more choice and options we have, the more we evaluate their respective benefits and the higher we raise our expectations. Unfortunately, the consequences are not always positive. As Schwartz explains, "Expectations can get so high that no result will meet them, no matter how good it is."

In other words, if the market for meaningful experiences becomes one where customers constantly search for the best, the most intense, or the most novel experience, then these experiences are unlikely to make much difference to our business culture. If instead we put some effort in determining what type of meanings we really desire, and focus on finding those companies that can authentically meet that desire in a consistent and pervasive way, we may all have more reason to smile.

Index